My Solo Exchange Diary 1

(true) story & art
Nagata Kabi

Entry No. 1 — 3
Entry No. 2 — 15
Entry No. 3 — 31
Entry No. 4 — 43
Entry No. 5 — 55
Entry No. 6 — 69
Entry No. 7 — 83
Entry No. 8 — 99
Entry No. 9 — 111
Entry No. 10 — 123
Entry No. 11 — 135
Entry No. 12 — 151
Bonus Entry — 164

My name is Nagata Kabi.
BOW
Nice to meet you.

Three years after I made my debut as a manga artist under a different name, I was overwhelmed by the growing dread that things would fall apart--and I got desperate.
TH
UN
DOING GOOD
DOING OKAY
CAN'T DO THIS
100
50
0
BZZZT

So, I drew and released my story of hiring an escort.
MY LESBIAN EXPERIENCE WITH LONELINESS
GRAAAI-!
CRASH
And doing that...
※ METAPHOR

somehow led to work.
?!

I got a series.
A SERIES!

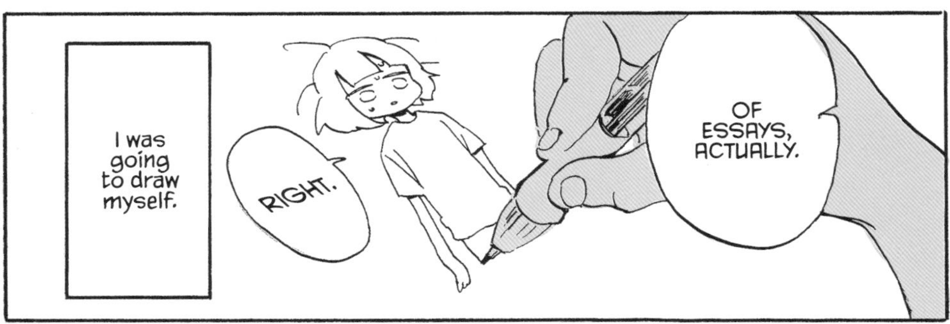
OF ESSAYS, ACTUALLY.
RIGHT.
I was going to draw myself.

UNNNNH!
WHAT AM I GONNA DO?
WHAT SHOULD I DRAW...?

I THOUGHT ABOUT IT FOR AN ENTIRE MONTH, BUT COULDN'T DECIDE ON ANYTHING.
And at a time like that...

That became my new direction.

HEEEY! JUNIOR HIGH SCHOOL *MEEEE!*

EVEN AFTER FOURTEEN YEARS, I'M STILL DOING THE EXCHANGE DIARY THING *ALOOONE!!*

I know you might feel bewildered right now, but I hope you'll enjoy it a little, at least.

I'm sorry for bringing this up right away, but my bank balance is a big fat zero.

THE PAYMENT FOR YOUR MONTHLY MOBILE PHONE PLAN COULD NOT BE WITHDRAWN FROM YOUR BANK ACCOUNT. PLEASE PAY THE BALANCE BEFORE THE 15TH TO KEEP SERVICE.

AAAAAH!!

※ NO EXPECTED INCOME FOR SEVERAL MONTHS.

*Money given to children on New Year's Day.

*About $10,000 USD.

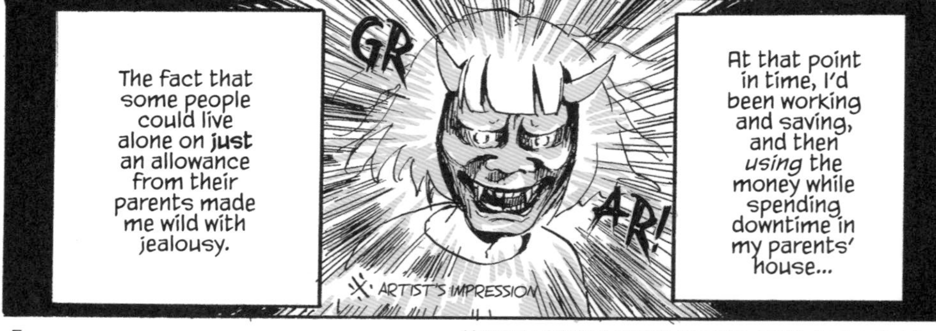

*A young adult that is "Not in Education, Employment, or Training."

When I used up my savings without ever moving out, I was surprised by the lingering effect that had on me.

I wanted to live by myself on my savings.

I moved into a place that did weekly rentals, from December 24 to January 7...
since being with my family during the year-end holidays was always exhausting.

Except for a four-day, three-night school trip back in the day, I'd never been away from my family.
THE TEACHER'S COMING!
ARE YOU SERI-OUS?
CONSTANT FAMILY CONTACT AWARD

Do you have a "real life satisfaction ranking" like this inside you, too?
TIME WITH FRIENDS
ALONE (WORK)
ALONE (BORED)
FAMILY
NOW HERE!
I think it's stupid, though. And more than anything, I wonder what family really *is* to me.

Just as all of this was on my mind...
I'M COMING BACK TO OSAKA. LET'S GRAB A DRINK!
CHOOOOM
TIME WITH FRIENDS
ALONE (WORK)
ALONE (BORED)
FAMILY
a friend from high school emailed me, and we decided to meet up.

Look, I hadn't seen my friends in three years.
CLAP...
I NATURALLY BROUGHT MY HANDS TOGETHER IN PRAYER.
I wondered if the experience would kill me.

Today, I'm not scared of the delighted people who squeal at each other when they're reunited.
SNORT
SNORT
SQUEE
They can scream and get carried away as much as they want.

OOOH, IT'S BEEN AGES~!
......
YOU DON'T LOOK SO GREAT, HUH?
SQUEE
Just like that...

I had managed to move out on someone else's dime...
...and unlock the achievement of *going for drinks with a friend* on someone else's dime.

I got to hear about our classmates, outside the few people I can check on social media. That was nice.
○○ WENT TO INDIA.
○○ DID, TOO.
The high ratio of people going to India was a little surprising.

My classmates were living such intense lives. Some were in mysterious countries, some were no longer in this world at all...
○○ PASSED AWAY.
and I'd been completely oblivious while stuck at my parents' house, a thought which stunned me.

A few days later, I was invited to a surprise party.
MARRIED FRIENDS WHO JUST CAME BACK TO JAPAN.
WELCOME BACK!
I SEE PHOTOS OF THIS ON TWITTER ALL THE TIME!
I went to it. They even had cake there.

And I went drinking again at the beginning of the year.
Afterward, I had my cozy little apartment to return to and work in.

All of it was covered by someone else's money (New Year's cash from childhood, et cetera).
IT'S 2,800 YEN EACH.
I HAVE CHANGE.

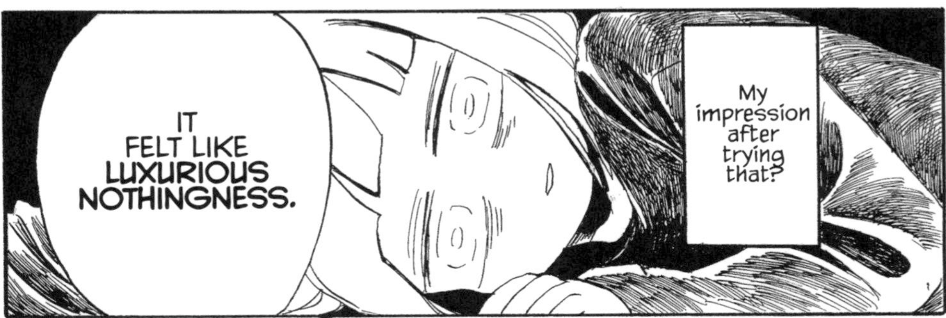
My impression after trying that?
IT FELT LIKE LUXURIOUS NOTHINGNESS.

I'd been so jealous longing for *something*--but not the "living alone on an allowance" part.
TAKE CARE OF YOURSELF AND WORK HARD, OKAY?
THANKS.
I'd wanted to be able to *accept* the allowance and have healthy relationships to spend it on.

But that's not possible for me, so I want to earn my own money and live my own life.
What will I be doing in the future? Can I really earn my own money?

My
Solo
Exchange
Diary

My
Solo
Exchange
Diary

Entry No. 2

Dear Nagata Kabi...
DEAR NAGATA KABI
FROM: NAGATA KABI
Hello, it's been a while. This is Nagata Kabi.

You (New Year's holiday me) seem to be having a lot of fun.
I'm in no position for that, now...

I still haven't managed to earn any money myself.
CHOMP
CHOMP
CHOMP
CHOMP
THANKS, FAMILY!
It's gonna be a while before I'm paid for the work I'm doing now. But I still have my New Year's money!

Anyway, have you ever gotten so lonely that your body grows cold and you can't move anymore?
I assume you don't. Because this is the first time it's happened to me.

I'M HOME...
In January, as planned, I went back to my parents' house because my mother had to spend some time in the hospital.

For a while, it was just my father and me.
My grand-mother and aunt came on the weekends.

I would wake up in the afternoon or sometime in the evening, do laundry, go see my mother at the hospital, do laundry, and work outside.

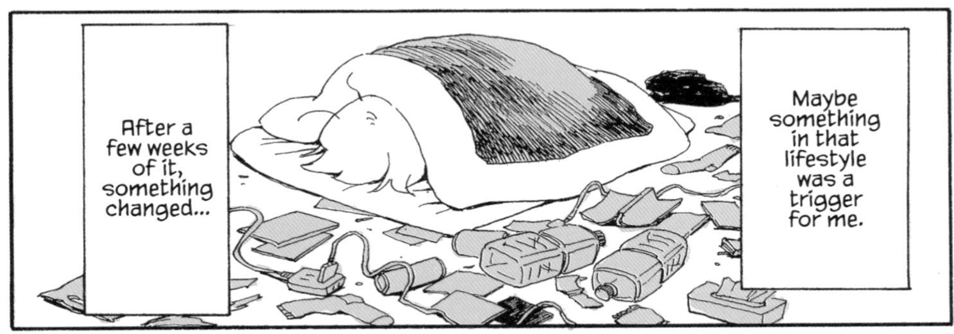
Maybe something in that lifestyle was a trigger for me.
After a few weeks of it, something changed...

I couldn't get up, but I couldn't sleep, either. And even if I managed to sleep, I still felt exhausted, somehow.
I felt more sluggish and tired than usual.

I felt like I was made of holes.
....
POK
POK
CHEESE
My breathing was sluggish, too--so it was hard to breathe. My chest hurt.

UNNH...
SQUEEZE
....

When I hugged my stuffed animals, my chest got ice cold and hurt even more.
PWUMP

No matter what I did, I couldn't warm up.
APPARENTLY, YOU'RE NOT SUPPOSED TO DO THIS...
BATH
HEATER
FUTON DRYER
WHRR
Every part of me started going cold.

SLEEPY. SLUGGISH. HURTS. COLD.
HURTS. COLD. TIRED. COLD. HARD.
COLD. COLD.
It started to affect my life and my work.

OH!
RIGHT.
THE PUBLIC BATH WARMS ME UP MORE THAN THE ONE IN THE HOUSE, FOR SOME REASON.

I started going to the public bath.

The water never gets cold there. It simmers you into warmth.
More than anything else, it was both nice and a pleasant change to get in the bath with strangers, totally naked and with naked eyes (of less than 20/20 vision).

When I got in the bath and closed my eyes, listening to all those voices in that world...
it felt like the walls between people infinitely approached zero, and my heart was warmed, too.

But a few days later...
?!
H- HUH...?
I'M COLD AGAIN!!

Whether the bath was booked for a private event or full of people...
......
the core of my heart stayed completely chilled. My body wouldn't warm up at all, anymore.

△◎
□●
◆〒
#¥
!!$
□〒
×※
△!!
■
?
I don't usually get it when my body and mind are yelling at me that we're sick.

My heart and body were screaming at me that we were lonely, that everything was too much.
LONELY.
LONELY.
LONELY.
LONELY.
But that many symptoms were too hard to ignore.

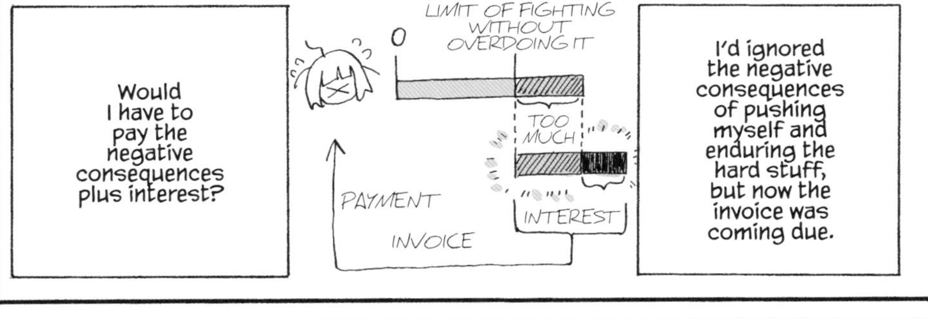
I'd ignored the negative consequences of pushing myself and enduring the hard stuff, but now the invoice was coming due.
0
LIMIT OF FIGHTING WITHOUT OVERDOING IT
TOO MUCH
PAYMENT
INVOICE
INTEREST
Would I have to pay the negative consequences plus interest?

It wasn't just for stuff I'd ignored the past few weeks, either--this was interest on my entire past.
WHAT HAVE YOU DONE?!
BILL
Current me got the bill.

IT'S GETTING IN THE WAY OF WORK, TOO. I HAVE TO DO SOMETHING-- AND QUICK.
I WANNA BE WITH PEOPLE AND WARM UP.
IS THERE ANYONE I CAN BE WITH? THERE HAS TO BE **SOMEONE.** I MEAN...
NO. NO, THERE'S... NO ONE.

THEN MY ONLY CHOICE IS TO RESOLVE THIS WITH MONEY.
I COULD GO BACK TO THAT ESCORT AGENCY I WROTE MY REPORT ON.
MY LESBIAN EXPERIEN WITH LONELINESS
WILL THAT GET RID OF MY LONELI-NESS?

ARE YOU GONNA GO PAY SOMEONE WHO DOESN'T LOVE YOU AND END UP FEELING EMPTY?!
AAAAAH!
YOU'RE RIPPING ME APART!!
LONELY, LONELY, LONELY! NO MORE, NO MORE, NO MORE, NO MORE!!

UNNNNH...
I SERIOUSLY HAVE TO DO SOME-THING...!

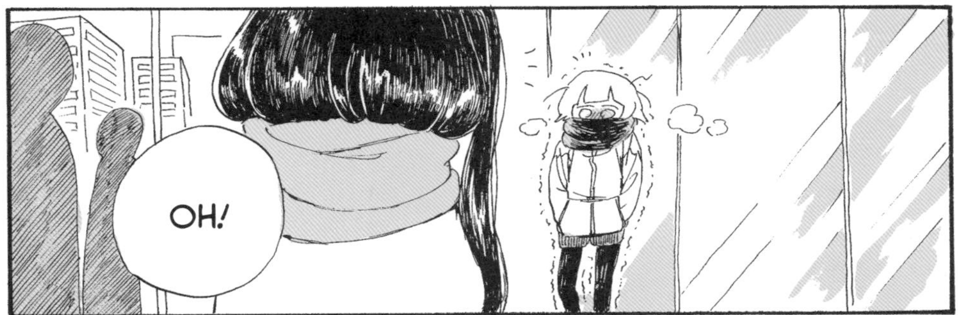

I came to the conclusion that there was no other solution, so I made an appointment with a girl from the escort agency.

UH. UM.
YES?
I WORK AT HOME, SO I DON'T EVER SEE PEOPLE... AND, LIKE, I'M KINDA DESPERATE FOR HUMAN CONTACT.
SURE, I UNDER-STAND.

IF YOU COULD HOLD ME TIGHT...
THAT WOULD MAKE ME REALLY HAPPY.

WELL, SURE!
WE CAN DO THAT!

WE'LL DO A LOT OF THAT!

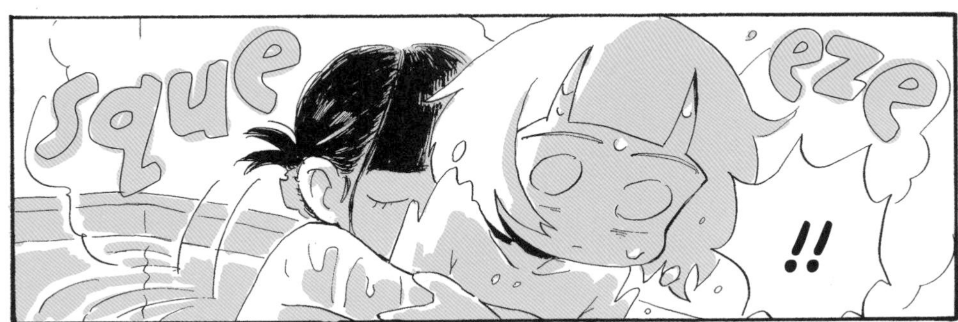

It was just that one comment, so I figured she'd forget about it.

She really did hug me a lot.
squeeeeeeeeze
NGAAH!

KISS
To go off on a little tangent, I realized something at that time.

IT'S LIKE...
THERE'S TOO MUCH INFORMATION.

OH, RIGHT. IS THIS WHY PEOPLE GO THROUGH STAGES WITH LOVE?

If you move seriously through the stages when facing another person...

you probably get a lot more out of it.

Like, if a grade school kid reads a high school textbook, what percentage of that information will they really be able to pick up?

I think right now I can only understand a certain amount, and the rest of it just gets lost.

But just like how you can write a book in simple words that moves the heart...

being squeezed tightly was still a huge comfort for me.

Later, I saw someone on Twitter say,

"Escort agencies are an extreme. Lots of people are satisfied with physical contact, even without the orgasm."

Which made me remember this experience.

When we got out of the bath after that, I saw my face in the mirror, and it was bright red-- but I still didn't realize what was happening.
RED ?!!
I HAAATE IT...
I GUESS IT'S PRETTY COLD OUT!

......
?!

I'd been freezing when I came to meet her, but I left so warm that my body was practically steaming.
I'M SO HOT, I DON'T EVEN NEED THIS SCARF?!
steam
WHAT?! I'M NOT COLD AT ALL!!
steam

My entire trip back, and even after I got home, I was a pocket of heat.

People with close friends or lovers or spouses can do this kind of thing, huh? And if you don't have anyone like that, your thoughts turn cold...

It was a little late for the thought, but that concept struck me as kinda unfair.

I hope I can find someone like that someday (as soon as possible, really)!

SO COLD!

BY THE WAY, THE EFFECT HUMAN SKIN HAS ON ANOTHER DOESN'T LAST THAT LONG.

Please work hard to become independent for that, too!

KRR

RR

My
Solo
Exchange
Diary

My
Solo
Exchange
Diary

Entry No. 3

Dear Nagata Kabi...
Hello. This is Nagata Kabi.
DEAR NAGATA KABI
FROM. NAGATA KABI

I've finally left home.

I've attained my greatest desire of the last ten years: I'm living alone.
YOU WON'T BE ABLE TO RENT ANYTHING WITH JUST A PART-TIME JOB.
DON'T BE FOOLED.
CAN YOU REALLY HANDLE THE HOUSE-WORK?
DAD
MOM
It took so long. So, so long...

So long, in fact...
POINT-LESS.
USE-LESS.
DON'T WASTE YOUR MONEY.
DAD
that I was left with no strong feelings about the matter at all.

I'd hit my limit.
MANU-SCRIPT
MANU-SCRIPT
MOVE HOUSE
LAUN-DRY
MOVE HOUSE
MANU-SCRIPT
MANU-SCRIPT
LAUN-DRY
I did wonder if I really needed to do it now, while I was working on two different manuscripts. But...

It's loneliness.
FEELING FULL OF HOLES AND NOTHING ELSE.
Just like you said last time...

I was lonelier when I was with my family.
DAD
GRAND-MA
AUNT
0
LONELINESS
I hadn't been lonely at all when I was on my own in the weekly rental.
0
LONELINESS

I looked for a place so I could leave the second she got back.
Since they told me to stay at home until my mother was discharged from the hospital...

RESTAURANT
IT'S ACTUALLY HARDER TO FIND SOMETHING WHEN THE LOCATION DOESN'T MATTER, HUH?
OH.
IT'S ALREADY ELEVEN? I WISH I DIDN'T HAVE TO GO HOME, BUT I SHOULD.

I'M HOME...
KA-CHAK
IT'S ABOUT TIME!
YOU CAN'T BE OUT THIS LATE.
WHAT?

THIS IS MUCH TOO LATE!!
BE HOME BY NINE.
"NINE"?! I'M TWENTY-EIGHT YEARS OLD!! TWENTY-EIGHT!!!

NIIIIINE ?!!
EVEN JUNIOR HIGH KIDS GOING TO CRAM SCHOOL CAN'T MAKE IT HOME THAT EARLY!
RIGHT...
Even with him worrying about me, I was still lonely. I did think he was concerned because he cared about me. So why was my heart cold and in such pain?

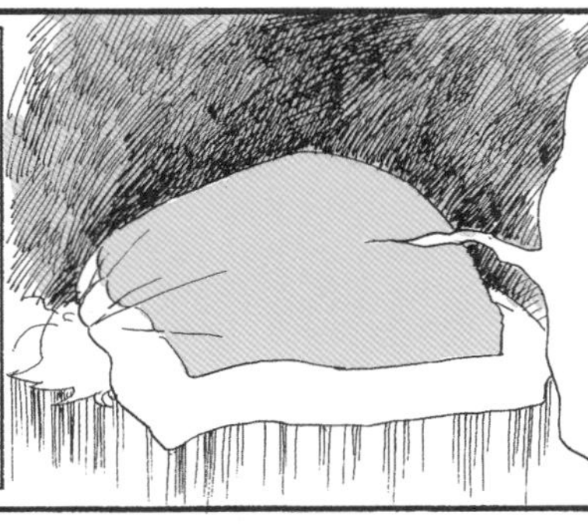
I SERIOUSLY CAN'T LIVE LIKE THAT, WITH THEM GETTING MAD AT ME IF I'M OUT LATER THAN NINE...

In the weekly rental, I'd stayed out even later with friends over the New Year's holidays.

I'M MOVING OUT.
POP

I found an apartment online that looked good, but it turned out it was just bait to get me into the office.
ALL THE REAL ESTATE AGENCIES ARE DOING THINGS LIKE THAT.
REALLY?
So, I found another decent-looking place...

and I applied for it, since it was good enough.
OH.
WHAT SHOULD I DO...
DAD
GUARANTOR:
DATE OF BIRTH:
PLACE OF EMPLOYMENT:
EMPLOYER PHONE #:
INCOME:
YEARS AT CURRENT EMPLOYER:
I'M SO UNINTERESTED IN MY PARENTS, THE ONLY THING I KNOW ABOUT HIM IS HIS NAME...

PRRING
PRRING...
OH!
HELLO?
HI, DAD. I'M WITH THE REAL ESTATE AGENT.
HOW DO YOU WRITE YOUR EMPLOYER'S INFO? LIKE, IS THERE AN OFFICE NUMBER?
WHAT ?!

SIGH
ARE YOU STILL FIXATED ON ALL THAT?

WHAT? Y-YEAH.
UM, YOUR EMPLOYER... AT HOME, OKAY...
O-OFFICE NUMBER... NONE. RIGHT.

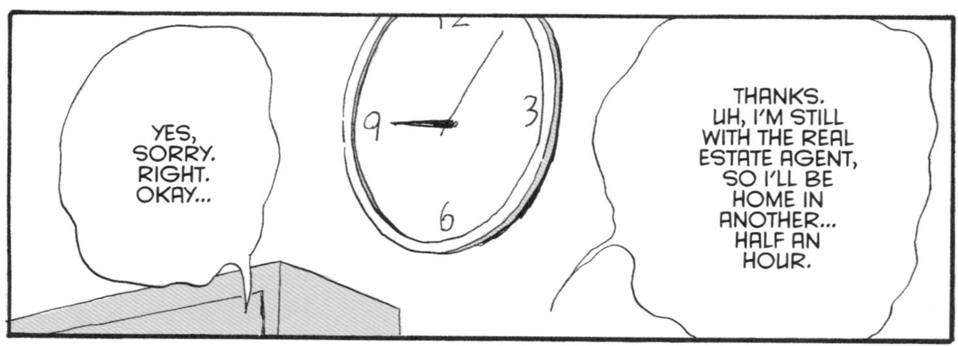
THANKS. UH, I'M STILL WITH THE REAL ESTATE AGENT, SO I'LL BE HOME IN ANOTHER... HALF AN HOUR.
YES, SORRY. RIGHT. OKAY...

I com-
plained
to my
mom
in the
hospital.
WHY
DON'T YOU
TRY TALKING
TO YOUR
FATHER? ♬
HUH
...?

QUIET.
SHUT
YOUR
MOUTH.
ENOUGH
OF
THIS.
DAD
YOU CAN'T
HAVE A
CONVERSATION
WITH HIM! WHAT
A RIDICULOUS
THING FOR HER
TO SAY AFTER
EVERYTHING
THAT'S
HAPPENED!

Before
that,
when I
had
talked
with my
mom...
I FEEL
LONELIER
WITH DAD
THAN I DO
WHEN I'M
ALONE.

I KNOW
WHAT
YOU
MEAN.
That's
what
she
said!
YOU
UNDER-
STAND,
RIGHT?

WE'RE IN A STATE OF EMERGENCY RIGHT NOW.
THE LEAST YOU CAN DO IS HELP YOUR FAMILY OUT A LITTLE.
DAD
OKAY.
I SET THE MOVE-IN DATE SO IT'S AFTER MOM COMES HOME.

SIIIIIGH...
YOU'RE GIVING ME A REAL CASE OF DEPRESSION HERE.

"YOU'RE GIVING ME A REAL...
CASE OF DEPRESSION HERE."

I honestly couldn't let that one slide.

After my dad left the room, I freaked out as quietly as possible.

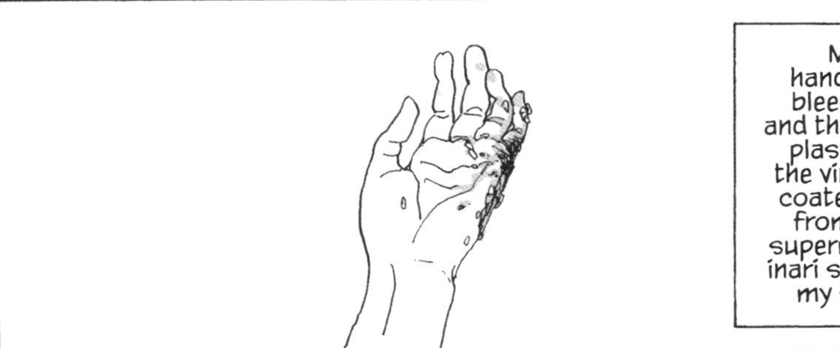

In the comments I got from *My Lesbian Experience* on pixiv...

"I THINK LONELINESS ISN'T BEING PHYSICALLY ALONE--IT'S WHEN THE PEOPLE AROUND YOU DON'T RECOGNIZE WHO YOU ARE OR YOUR ABILITIES."

And then, after all that effort...
WHAT?!
I DIDN'T GET ANYTHING LIKE THAT.
my father apparently hadn't taken me seriously, so he hadn't gathered the paperwork I'd asked for.

I got my key long, long after the move-in date I wanted.
I CAN'T BELIEVE IT TOOK THIS MUCH TIME.

Bottom line: there was no way I could muster any feeling at that point.
I'M TIRED.
The day I got the key to the long-awaited apartment...

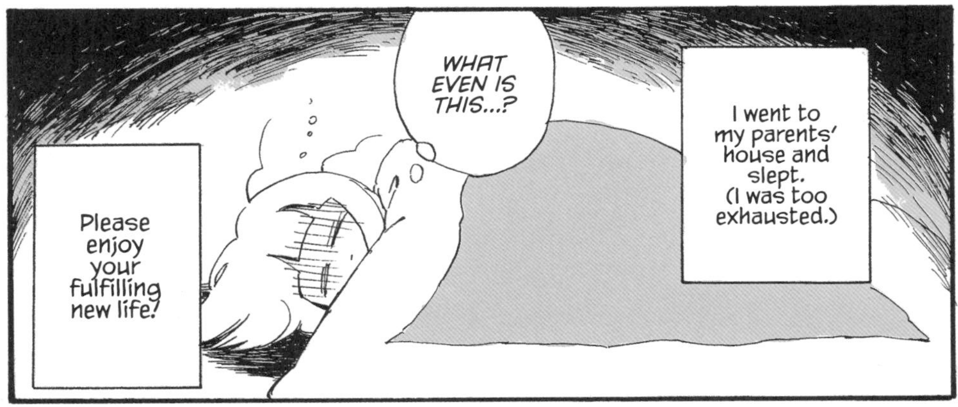
I went to my parents' house and slept. (I was too exhausted.)
WHAT EVEN IS THIS...?
Please enjoy your fulfilling new life!

My
Solo
Exchange
Diary

My
Solo
Exchange
Diary

Entry No. 4

Hello. This is Nagata Kabi.
DEAR NAGATA KABI
FROM: NAGATA KABI
Dear Nagata Kabi...
Congratulations on your move so you can finally live alone.
I want to apologize to you (past me) for something.
I'm sorry...
FLOP

This is really hard to say, but...

you can't live in your new place!

AT MY PARENTS' HOUSE!

I couldn't turn it into something livable in my spare time between manuscripts.
SCATTERING

ONE OF MY FOLLOWERS IS LIVING ALONE, HUH...?
WOW...
I'M SAD ABOUT LEAVING THE FAMILY CAT BEHIND...
WHEN DID YOU MOVE OUT?
APRIL!
NICE. LUCKY~!

WAIT, WHAT?
I'd moved out, but I was still jealous of someone else getting their own place.

I worked hard to make things nicer, but...
THE AIR CONDITIONER MAKES A WEIRD NOISE, AND IT KEEPS BLOWING COLD AIR WHEN I SET IT TO WARM.
COLD AIR
WHD KRR
WHD KRR
WHD KRR
WHD KRR
WHD KRR
KRR

COLD AIR
THE WALLS ARE REALLY THIN. I COULD PROBABLY HAVE A CONVERSATION THROUGH THEM.
BARK BARK
STOP THAT!

I knew rushing my decision was a bad idea!!
I'LL GO WITH THAT PLACE FROM BEFORE.
HURRY AND MOVE. HURRY, HURRY, MOVE.
HURRY, HURRY. HURRY AND MOVE. HURRY AND MOVE.
REALLY?
ALL RIGHT...
Well, I totally understand that sense of urgency.

....
I'M MOVING.
I JUST MOVED HERE...
BUT I'M GOING TO GO BEFORE I NEED THE AIR CONDITIONER.

I FEEL BAD FOR THE PEOPLE WHO HELPED AND CONGRATULATED ME, THOUGH. THEY'LL PROBABLY LOSE FAITH IN ME.
HUH ...?!

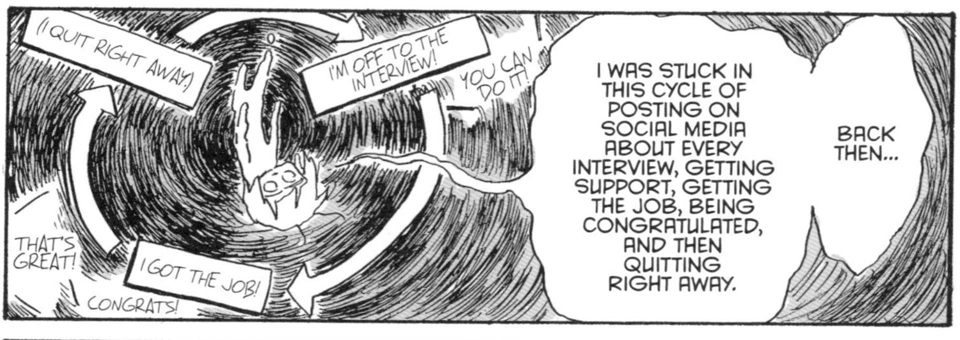

EVEN THOUGH I WAS MAKING TROUBLE FOR MYSELF *AND* THE PEOPLE AT MY JOB, EVEN THOUGH I WAS AFRAID OF LOSING HUMANITY'S TRUST... I COULDN'T STOP.

Back then, I did have countermeasures to break free of the "quitting jobs" cycle.

I wasn't getting paid as much, but at least I didn't need to worry about all of humanity losing faith in me.

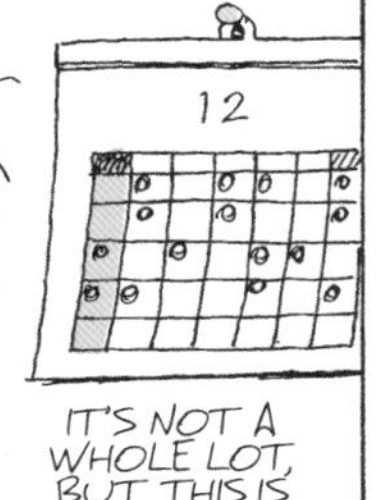

I think I was just... really thorough about running a mental scenario to see if I could do something, then only accepting things I could actually handle.

"Taking responsibility" includes **only** attempting things you know you can manage.

I recognized the difference between my *actual* abilities and the abilities of the imaginary me who could magically do more.

With my jobs, the move, and probably other stuff, I cause all these problems for other people. It never goes smoothly, and it's exhausting for me, too.

To keep from falling into a loop where people lose faith in me again, I just have to apply that theory to my moving plans.
I'LL THINK HARD ABOUT WHETHER I REALLY *COULD* LIVE THERE FIRST!
I'LL ASK OTHER PEOPLE TO HELP WITH THE STUFF THAT'S OVER MY LIMIT!
!
AHHH~! THAT WAS CLOSE. WHAT A CLOSE CALL!
I WAS ON THE VERGE OF LOSING A LOT OF MONEY AND HUMANITY'S FAITH IN ME.
......
NO, NO, NO, *NOOOOO!* WHY DO I HAVE TO ALMOST LOSE EVERYTHING FIRST?!
PAY ATTENTION *BEFORE* YOU START THE CYCLE!!
I at least want to tell my future self that you can't make a decision based on just the rent and whether the bath and toilet are separate.
PLEASE! PLEASE!
I'M BEGGING YOU!
Think hard about what you actually want.

I mean, I wasn't getting help from anyone or making any investments, and I couldn't rely on myself...

not even when I was on breaks from the manuscripts...

PEOPLE & PLACES TO RELY ON

INVESTMENT IN MYSELF

RELATIONSHIPS WITH PEOPLE

I want future me to be an independent person who relies on others *appropriately* and can be relied on in the same way.

INDEPENDENT!

I want to be someone who gets help from people and repays it, who's built up relationships with people outside her family.

NOW

My
Solo
Exchange
Diary

My
Solo
Exchange
Diary

Entry No. 5

Dear Nagata Kabi...
Hello. This is Nagata Kabi.

It's May. I'm still at my parents' house.

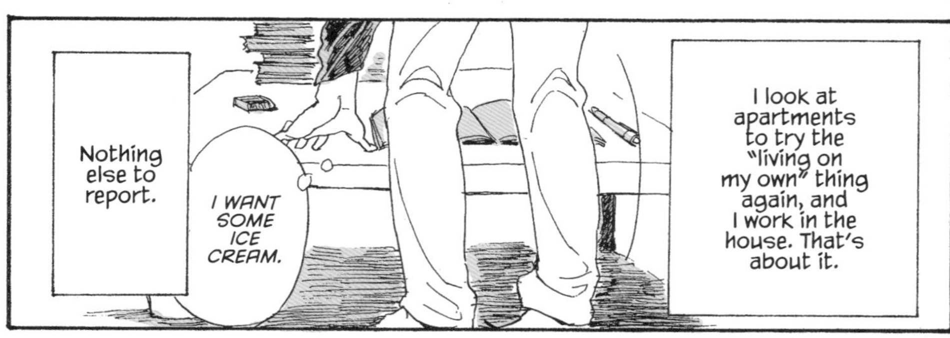
I look at apartments to try the "living on my own" thing again, and I work in the house. That's about it.
I WANT SOME ICE CREAM.
Nothing else to report.

This time...
KA-SHUNK
I want to talk about a thought I had lately.

I was thinking "happiness" is basically "something in this current world that lacks unhappiness."

Maybe you could also say it's "not acknowledging unhappiness."

Or "not imagining unhappiness." Or just "letting go of it."

The times when you think, "I'm so happy right now!" occur when you're only thinking about the good stuff.

It's a state where you ignore the stuff that could spoil your happiness--no matter what's happening at the time.

Looking at it so shrewdly might actually ruin your happiness...

but that's just the way it works.

Conversely, if you're anxious or depressed or exhausted...
it can feel like there's only unhappiness in the world.

Right at this very moment, people everywhere are dealing with terrifying things. It's almost dizzying.
Maybe you just happened to be different, is all.

There are missing people out there and people who are looking for them, sleepless with worry...
while others still are taking advantage of them.

There are scared people and people who think they'd be better off dead...
Right now. Right in this very neighbor-hood.

On the other side of that window, there could be a gruesome crime scene.

...!

It's not that they're wrong in thinking like that.
Something fun!
IT'S PRETTY HARD NOT TO THINK ABOUT, THOUGH.
But constantly thinking about that kind of thing gets in the way of life, so people just **don't** think about it.

ALL RIGHT! YUMMY!
When you're "happy," you take information in selectively. Your field of vision is incredibly narrow.

There's a powerful attractive force at my parents' house--plus another force that makes it impossible to move away. I realized that again after I came back.

Changing the topic, I have one more thought.

Until a few years ago, I thought the pain in my life was all because of my mother.

Only recently did I realize that that wasn't the case.

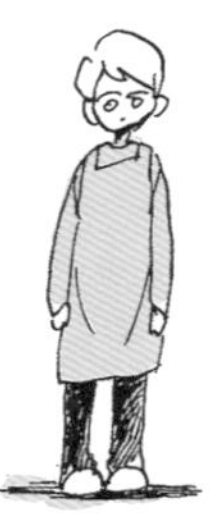

She's lost the confidence to go out and work... I wonder why I didn't notice it all before.
YOU HAVE A DUTY TO CARE FOR ME UNTIL I DIE.
She gets bullied by her mother-in-law, who lives with us. There's no mutual respect in the house.

Not only is my mother **not** to blame, but she's a victim herself.

Maybe *everyone's* a victim in some way.
It seems like there are a lot of reports about how even people deemed "criminals" were victims when they were young.
XXXX SUSPECT

So... is it really okay to leave her alone in this house?
My helpless mother got married even though she suspected something was off...

What's gonna happen to her when she has no allies in this house?

And when I *do* leave home, will I really be free if I'm still carrying that worry around?

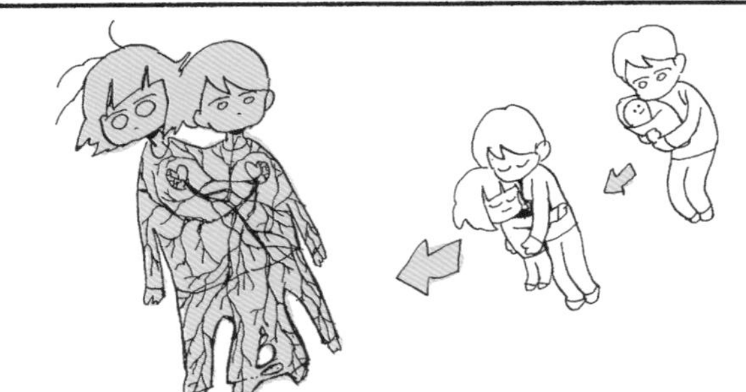

We've been glued together forever, to the point where we can't pull apart.

If I'm pulled in by the house, unable to abandon my mother...

then won't I just come back, no matter how many times I leave?

……
HAPPINESS IS... IGNORING YOUR UNHAPPINESS. ABANDONING IT.
MY HAPPINESS IS...
ABANDONING MY MOTHER.
That was when I learned that you can reject something you know to be true.
All my thoughts on the matter tried to dissipate like mist.

I truly understood that apart from being **unable** to be happy...

past me had always wished for my mother's happiness.

I can only move forward and live my own life how I want to live it.

I can't let anyone else be part of this exchange diary, either.

To improve my own life and happiness...

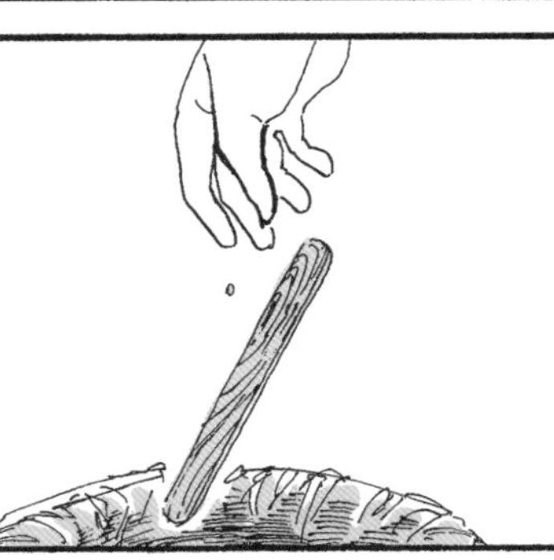

I have to wash my hands of the nearby despair that I can't do anything about.

Although, I don't really believe that.
HAPPY
I'm going to believe that she **will** find happiness.

MOM
VVOOOOOOOOOM
AAAAH!
Future me, you'll probably be dragged back again by the attraction of this house and the attachment to my mother.

Please think about that, and please... fight.

Maybe "living" is just repeating that over and over.
I'm sorry to ask you for something so aggravating, but I know you can do it.

!

THE INSURANCE COMPANY INSPECTION IS FINISHED, SO...
OH...! THIS IS GREAT!

....
THIS TIME I'M LEAVING HOME FOR *SURE*...!!

MOM, I JUST WANT YOU TO BE HAPPY, BUT...
AAH, IT'S SO HARD. IT HURTS.
IT'S TOO HOT FOR THAT, *UGH!* STOP IT!
Please do your best at living alone... and make it last this time.

My
Solo
Exchange
Diary

My
Solo
Exchange
Diary

Entry No. 6

Dear Nagata Kabi...
Hello. This is Nagata Kabi.

Thanks to you, I decided on an apartment.
WHAT SORT OF MANGA DO YOU DRAW?
I signed a lease without any trouble this time.

And then, at the end of May...
SOLO EXCHANGE DIARY
NAGATA KABI
I finally started this series on pixiv Comics.

The first chapter was published in the magazine *Hibana*, too. A copy of that magazine...
arrived at my parents' house.

This was on the first page.
They also ran an ad for *My Lesbian Experience with Loneliness* along with it.
CAN DO ALL SORT
OF GIRL ON GIRL
STUFF
MY LESBIAN EXPERIEN
WITH LONELINES
ON SALE JUNE
CRASH

And it was delivered to my parents' house.
ARE YOU IN THAT?
JOLT

....
I'M... NOT. (I AM.)

While writing under another name, I'd pulled the "I'm not in this" scam a lot, so she was pretty suspicious.
REALLY?!
BUT YOU ACTUALLY *ARE* IN IT, AREN'T YOU?!

YOU'RE NOT DRAWING MANGA ANYMORE?
HUH?! NO, UM...!
I AM. FOR ME, I'M DRAWING A LOT!!
I obviously hadn't shown her the pixiv version of *My Lesbian Experience*, but I also hadn't shown her a single thing I'd drawn after that under the name "Nagata Kabi."

I REMEMBER THAT MEETING YOU WENT TO. HOW DID *THAT* PROJECT GO?
WHEN DOES IT COME OUT?
WAAAAAH!
I'M NOT LYING!
I WASN'T SAYING YOU WERE...
But in order to show her I was working, I couldn't keep it a *complete* secret.

WHAAAT? REALLY?
DA
SH
PANIC PANIC
SHFF SHFF
I'M OKAY WITH IT, BUT MOM COULDN'T HANDLE THIS! I CAN'T SHOW HER!!

Incidentally, my editor-- for whom I'd drawn several one-shots under a pen name-- was **also** not told.
(TEXT MESSAGE)
WITH THE MOMENTUM YOU'VE GOT, YOU SHOULD HURRY AND SEND THE NEXT THUMBNAILS.
THEY THINK I'M JUST SKIPPING OUT ON MY WORK!!

HUFF!
HUFF!
WHEN I'M NOT WORKING, THEY SAY SCARY THINGS TO ME.
WHEN I *AM* WORKING, THEY TELL ME TO SHOW THEM.
SHOWING THE WORK TO THEM WOULD BE SCARY, TOO.
BUT THEY GET MAD AT ME IF I DON'T SHOW THEM...

AAAUGH...
SLUMP...
I WANNA MOVE OUT ALREADY.

I HAVE DEADLINES AND NEED TO PACK. I CAN'T MOVE OUT SOONER. MAGAZINES ARE BEING DELIVERED TO MY HOUSE.
MY LESBIAN EXPERIENCE WITH LONELINESS
FORMAT: MANGA
¥ 999
THE BOOK COVER GOES LIVE ONLINE AT THE END OF MAY, TOO.

IT'S A BATTLE AGAINST TIME...
TO TRY TO MAKE A CLEAN GET-AWAY!!

UNNNH...
I'M EXHAUSTED. THIS IS SO HARD...
IN POOR CONDITION EVERY DAY.
....

YOU MIGHT FEEL BETTER IF YOU QUIT MANGA.
WHISPER

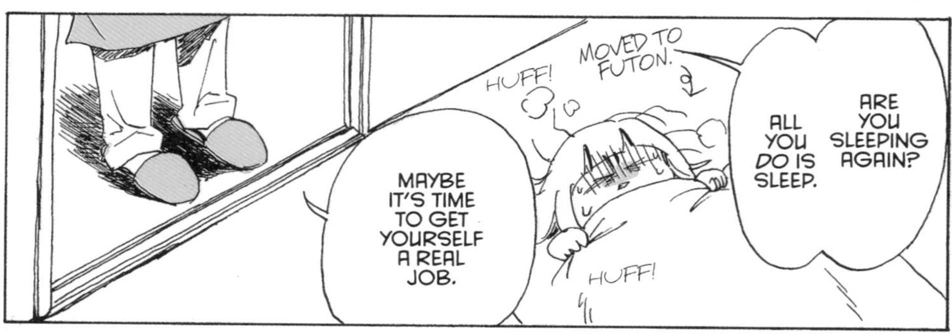
ARE YOU SLEEPING AGAIN?
ALL YOU DO IS SLEEP.
MOVED TO FUTON.
HUFF!
MAYBE IT'S TIME TO GET YOURSELF A REAL JOB.
HUFF!

SLAM
TUP TUP TUP TUP TUP TUP...
STAIRS

I ran a poll on Twitter.

SHOW THEM JUST WHAT YOU CAN. 8%

SHOW THEM EVERYTHING. 2%

SHOW THEM ABSOLUTELY NOTHING. 22%

OTHER/VIEW RESULTS. 68%

1,122 VOTES/POLL CLOSED

The majority voted that I **not** show my parents the manga I was working on.

I sent Amazon links to my aunt (my mother's younger sister), to test if it would be okay to show my parents, too.
IF POSSIBLE, I WANT HER TO JUST ACCEPT IT AND SAY NICE THINGS TO ME.

YOU DEFINITELY CAN'T SHOW THIS TO GRANDMA AND GRANDPA, HM... (LOL)
REPLY

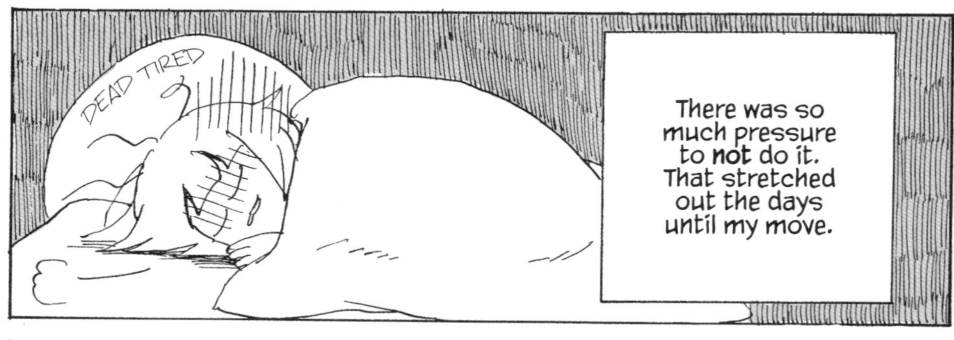
There was so much pressure to **not** do it. That stretched out the days until my move.
DEAD TIRED

THE NEXT MORNING.
—...
IT HURTS...

My mysteriously bad health hit rock bottom.
I'M EXHAUSTED, BUT I CAN'T SLEEP. IT HURTS. *I CAN'T.* HELP!

AH?!
WAIT... IS THIS PAIN BECAUSE I'M HIDING THINGS FROM MOM?!

I WANNA FEEL BETTER.
IT HURTS.

*NO, THIS IS ACTUALLY SOMETHING TO WRITE ABOUT. I **SHOULD** BE SHOWING HER! IT'S NOT WORTH MY MENTAL AND PHYSICAL HEALTH!!*
CLOP...
I CAN TOTALLY DO THIS!!

CREEP...
......
....
CREEP...
?

OH, YOU'RE GOING TO SHOW ME?
FLIP...
OR NOT...?

HUH...?
HUH?
....

DASH
AAAAAAAAAAH!!
....

I know in theory that this will be a topic to write about...
HUFF!
HUFF!
but I feel a brake being pulled, like I'm driving straight into danger.

IT'S NO USE! I *CAN'T*!!
WHY ?!
IT'S THAT BAD?! WHY IS THIS SO IMPOSSIBLE ...?!

YOU'RE SLEEPING *AGAIN?*
DON'T BE ASLEEP EVERY TIME I LOOK AT YOU.
....
YOU'RE EMBAR-RASSING THIS FAMILY...
AND DIS-GRACING YOUR PARENTS.

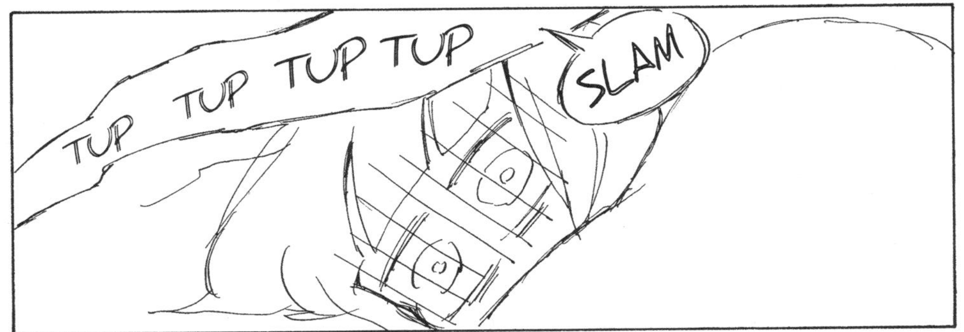
TUP TUP TUP TUP
SLAM

I wanted her to love me, no matter what I did.
I wanted my mom to say I was good just the way I was.

But ever since I'd realized that she really wasn't like that...
that lingering sense of *danger* had been slamming on my brakes.
?!

I'M SORRY FOR CONSTANTLY SAYING THAT YOU'RE PATHETIC, OR EMBARRASSING...
"I'M EMBARRASSED WHEREVER SHE SHOWS UP."
MY ABUSIVE WORDS
"PATHETIC."
"I WOULDN'T HAVE ANYTHING TO DO WITH HER IF SHE WASN'T MY MOTHER."
I DID THIS TO HER, TOO. I ALWAYS EXPECTED MORE FROM MY MOM.
NGH! NNGH!

BUT IF THEY'RE NOT GONNA ACCEPT THE CURRENT ME WHEN I'M LIVING WITH THEM, THEN I'M JUST ALONE.
I'M SO LONELY.
AAAH... I DON'T WANNA GO.

What I really wanted was for them to accept me and forgive me, and then I could stay in their house forever.
I DON'T CARE WHAT KIND OF PERSON YOU ARE.
I JUST WANTED YOU TO LOVE ME.

But in the end...
BUM
I couldn't proudly show her my work, even as it faced the world on Amazon.

On June 1, I moved.

This time, I did things right and hired a mover. The two of us were done in an hour.
I DON'T USUALLY GET THIS MUCH HELP.
TREMBLE
SHAKE
I had basically all the things I needed for a comfortable life.

Because I wanted to be a person who could use her own money to live nicely...
OOH...
and as motivation to stay there, I picked a stylish place where the rent was on the high side.
SO CHIC!
ORANGES
ALLLLL I HAVE TO WORRY ABOUT IS RENT!
SO COMFORTABLE~!!
ROLL
ROLL
ROLL
Now, just work hard to pay your rent! It's all on you, future me!!
This way, I can get through the sales of the book and the series without fear! Be grateful to me for that.
And please tell me one thing, future me...
Are you **happy** right now?

My
Solo
Exchange
Diary

MOM

I SAW YOUR SERIES. AND YOU WROTE ABOUT THE BOOK COVER ON TWITTER, SO I LOOKED. I HAVEN'T SAID ANYTHING ABOUT IT TO YOUR FATHER YET.

MOM 00:00

SHE MIGHT TELL DAD.
KREE KREE
KREE KREE
AND I'VE ALWAYS SHOWN THEM RIGHT AWAY BEFORE.
WAIT. BEFORE ANY KIND OF OPINION...
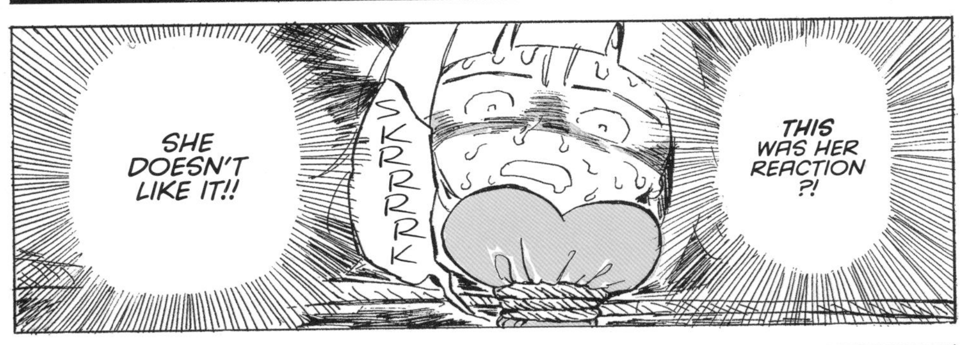
THIS WAS HER REACTION ?!
SKRRRK
SHE DOESN'T LIKE IT!!

OH, RIGHT.
DAD KNOWS SOMEONE WHO TOLD HIM ABOUT THE MAGAZINE.
SKRRRK
HE ALREADY KNOWS THE NAME OF IT.
THAT PERSON MIGHT SHOW IT TO DAD.

I'M WORRIED ABOUT THAT, TOO. HE DOESN'T NEED ANYONE OUTSIDE THE FAMILY TELLING HIM TO LOOK AT HIS OWN SHAME.
MOM 00:00

SHAME
WORRIED

IT'S ONLY A MATTER OF TIME BEFORE IT COMES OUT.
MOM 00:00
THE PROBLEM IS HOW TO TELL HIM.
MOM 00:00

I'M DRAWING IT AS A STORY.
I THINK PEOPLE WILL READ IT AS A NARRATIVE AND NOT AS GOSSIP ABOUT MY FAMILY. PROBABLY...
00:00
RIGHT. EVERY FAMILY HAS ITS OWN ISSUES.
MOM 00:00
NO, THAT'S NOT WHAT I'M SAYING...
IT'S MORE LIKE... ARE YOU EMBARRASSED **NOW** ABOUT THINGS THAT HAPPENED TO ME OVER THE COURSE OF A DECADE?
AND IT'S A BOOK.
WHAT ABOUT THE FACT THAT I PUT OUT A BOOK?

ALSO, YOU WROTE YOUR REAL NAME ON THE TWITTER, AND THE PERSON WHO GAVE ME THE MAIL WAS LOOKING PRETTY CLOSELY AT WHO IT WAS ADDRESSED TO. THEY KNOW SOME-ONE HERE WROTE IT.
WHAT?

N-NO, NO NO NO ...!
YOU'RE REALLY OVER-THINKING THIS!!
I...!!
SHUDDER
SHUDDER
SHUDDER
SHUDDER
SHUDDER
I HADN'T EVEN THOUGHT THAT FAR!

AND WHAT IS SHE SO UPSET ABOUT?!
IS WHAT I DREW SO WRONG?!

DID I DRAW SOME-THING SO WRONG?!
SO!! WRONG?!

I FEEL LIKE SHE'S GONNA SAY, "YOU DON'T NEED TO DRAW A TOPIC LIKE THAT. WHY DON'T YOU DRAW SOMETHING ELSE?"
AND I MEAN, I *WANT* TO DRAW FICTION OR SOME KIND OF COOL MANGA...
BUT WHAT I **WANT** TO DO AND WHAT I *CAN* DO ARE DIFFERENT.

At times like this, I often find the perfect Tweet for what I'm thinking.
OOOO @....
WHAT YOU WANT TO DO AND WHAT YOU CAN DO ARE DIFFERENT THINGS. I THINK "DOING WHAT YOU CAN" MAKES YOU A PRO, AND THEN YOU GROW TO LOVE IT.
YES! THIS!!

A PRO DOES WHAT THEY'RE CAPABLE OF...
STAGGER...
STAGGER
WELL, IT'S ALL GOOD AS LONG AS I UNDERSTAND THAT, AT LEAST. IT'S GOOD, BUT...

DON'T NITPICK EVERY LITTLE THING AND MESS ME UP.

On June 8, my comp copies arrived.
OOH!
KA-SNAP
KA-SNAP
INCLUDES BOOKS FOR SIGNING.

BLAH BLAH BLAH, SO PLEASE TELL ME YOUR ADDRESS.
UMM, I'LL SEND ONE TO MY EDITOR...
AND ONE TO THE EATING DISORDER COUNSELOR WHO HELPED ME.

IT'S BEEN A WHILE, BUT I REMEMBER YOU VERY WELL, KABI-SAN. YOU DID IT, HUH? HOORAY! I KNOW YOU WORKED HARD FOR IT.
SAN 00:00

THIS WAS ALL I WANTED! WAAAAAH!!
WAAAAAAAH!
THIS!! I JUST WANTED SOMEONE TO SAY SOMETHING LIKE THIS...!

I went to my parents' house on an errand and left a copy there.
THEY'LL FEEL IT WHEN THEY HAVE THE ACTUAL BOOK IN THEIR HANDS.
IT'S A REAL PUBLISHED WORK, AFTER ALL.
GIFTS

On my way home.
WHAT SHOULD I DO WITH THE BOOK? SHOULD I PUT IT ON YOUR FATHER'S CHAIR?
MOM 00:00

MOM 00:00
AND IF YOU DO PUT IT THERE?
00:00
I CAN'T TELL WHAT YOUR FATHER'S REACTION WILL BE, BUT I THINK HE SHOULD BE ABLE TO ACCEPT THE TRUTH.
I HAVE MY HANDS FULL WITH HIM, THE HOUSE, AND GRANDMA. SORRY I CAN'T PUT YOUR FEELINGS FIRST.
MOM 00:00
NUANCE IS HARD IN TEXT MESSAGES. LET'S MEET AND TALK ABOUT IT.
MOM 00:00
WE WERE TOGETHER IN PERSON FOR **TWENTY-EIGHT YEARS,** AND IT WAS HOPELESS. WHAT DO YOU EXPECT NOW?!
HA HA HA
HA HA HA
DO YOU THINK YOU'LL SUDDENLY "GET IT" IF WE MEET UP?!

The next day.
YOUR FATHER SAID SOMETHING ALONG THE LINES OF, "YOU'RE PROBABLY OVER THE MOON NOW THAT YOUR BOOK IS OUT, BUT IF YOU'RE FIXATED ON GETTING RECOGNITION FROM THE WORLD, YOU'LL HAVE TO GET TO WORK AGAIN RIGHT AWAY, AND YOU'LL BE EXHAUSTED FOREVER. I'VE ALWAYS SAID THIS, BUT THAT VALUE SYSTEM ISN'T EVERYTHING."
MOM 0:00

MAIL
DEAR AUNTIE,
AS SOMEONE WHO'S KNOWN ME FOR A LONG TIME, I'D LIKE TO HEAR YOUR UNBIASED AND NON-THREATENING OPINIONS.

From: AUNTIE
I READ IT! KABI'S GOOD. I MEAN, DRAWINGS LIKE THIS WILL DEFINITELY GET PEOPLE READING.

I was seriously relieved that I'd left home.

Thanks, past me! Good move!

After the release date on the seventeenth, reactions started to come in.
STARTING THE DAY WITH A SEARCH FOR MYSELF.

○○○ @''''
NAGATA KABI'S BOOK IS OUT! I GOT IT! SHE REVISED A LOT. IT'S GREAT!
△△△△ @''''
I WANT MY LESBIAN EXPERIENCE IN SCHOOLS AND STUFF. I THINK IT WOULD HELP SO MANY PEOPLE.
□□ @''''
NOT THE KIND OF "SEXY" YOU
EXPECT SUCH A GOOD
pic.twitter.com/......

CHEEP CHEEP...
CHIRP CHIRP

It was like...
waking up from a nightmare to see beautiful weather outside.

But even though I **knew** I'd be happier if I stepped out into that lovely weather...

Like a bucket full of holes, or a jar with the lid on.

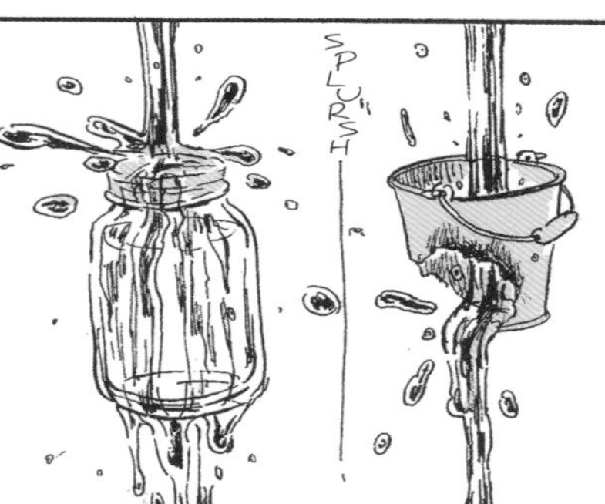

The happiness I'd supposedly been looking for was really pouring in... but it just spilled right out, and I stayed empty.

I JUST HAVE TO TAKE IT NOW! GO ON-- TAKE IT!
I MADE IT WITHOUT HAVING TO FACE THE NIGHTMARE (MY PARENTS), AND I'M GETTING THE GOOD REVIEWS I WANTED.

I **HATE** THE ME WHO'S STILL FIXATED ON MOM, EVEN WHILE SO MANY OTHER PEOPLE PRAISE ME! SHE SUCKS!!
AGH--

FORGET ABOUT HER!!
JUST GIVE IT UP, OKAY?! STOP GETTING HURT!
WHY ARE YOU OBSESSED WITH MOM?!

Please, as-soon-as possible me... get to a place where you can accept this joy.
At long last, I was facing the final stages of separation from my mother. (Is this really the end?)

My
Solo
Exchange
Diary

My
Solo
Exchange
Diary

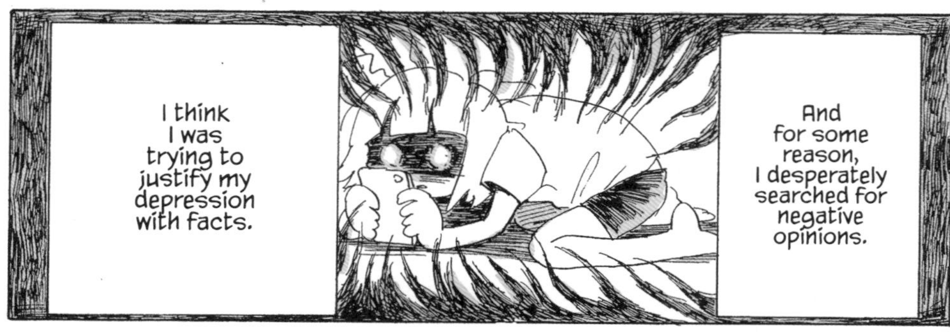

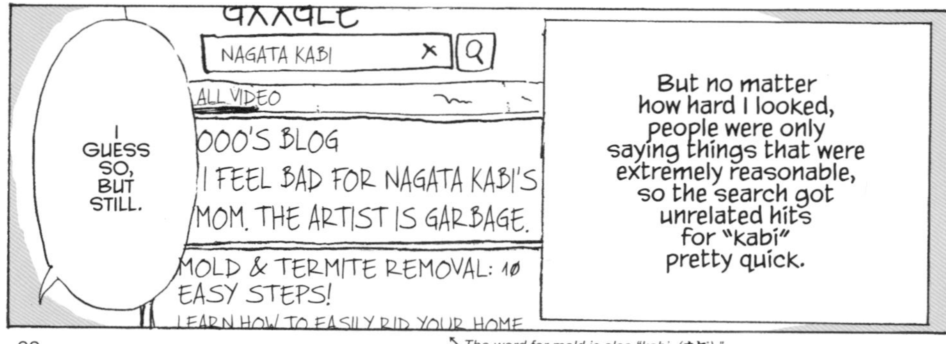

↖ *The word for mold is also "kabi (カビ)."*

But let's put that aside for now. Living alone is great, so let me tell you about it.
HEH HEH HEH...
The scary dream state continued in my head.

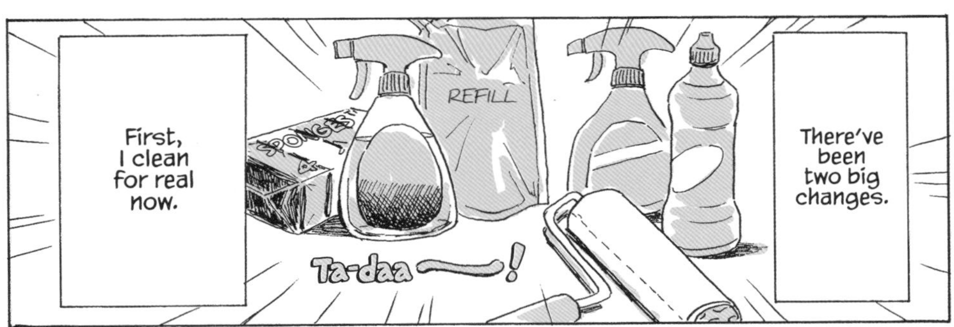
First, I clean for real now.
REFILL
Ta-daa—!
There've been two big changes.

Cleaning's become a habit when I can't concentrate--or after my deadlines.
Hmm hmm...
SQUEAK
SQUEAK
I can't believe it, either. It's part of what I do here.

HOW IS THAT DONE?!
DRIP
DRIP
ALL DONE.
SPLORSH
When I was at my parents' house, my cleanliness standards were... very different from theirs.

Eventually, I gave up on the whole endeavor and stopped cleaning altogether.
THERE'S STILL A DROP OF WATER THERE.
WHERE ?!

It's like that thing you hear about--the husband who doesn't wanna clean since his wife nitpicks him whenever he does.
WHY DON'T YOU CLEAN IF YOU'VE GOT NOTHING TO DO?
....
I DON'T WANT TO. YOU'LL JUST TELL ME I'M DOING IT WRONG.

Or like a bride who runs away, unable to endure her nagging mother-in-law.
I'M GOING BACK TO MY PARENTS' HOUSE!
AH, HEY! SHE'S GETTING AWAY!

No one was nitpicking me now, and if I wasn't cleaning enough, I was the one who suffered, so it was easy to tell.
THAT REEKS!
GROSS!
RIGHT, TIME TO CLEAN!!
SMELL FROM THE DRAIN.
I think it's good that I can do that stuff at my own pace, now.

And one more change.
7:45
I SLEPT AT NIGHT AND WOKE UP IN THE MORNING!!
I DID THAT YESTERDAY *AND* THE DAY BEFORE YESTERDAY, TOO!!
My life rhythm has sorted itself out.
When I was living at home, my days and nights weren't reversed, exactly.
... SLEEP TIME
NORMAL PERSON
12 0 12 0 12 0
ME
12 0 12 0 12 0
It was that "one day" wasn't twenty-four hours.
First of all, my sleeping and waking times were all over the place.
SO LOUD. I'M GONNA SLEEP...
1
2
BLAH! BLAH!
I also shifted my hours so I wouldn't run into people in the house. Those two things screwed up my Circadian rhythm.
My life had separated out into time I was "awake" or "asleep."
S-SUCH A HEALTHY LIFESTYLE...
FOR SOMEONE LIKE ME...
......
When my sleep schedule got knocked off, it started to naturally fix itself.

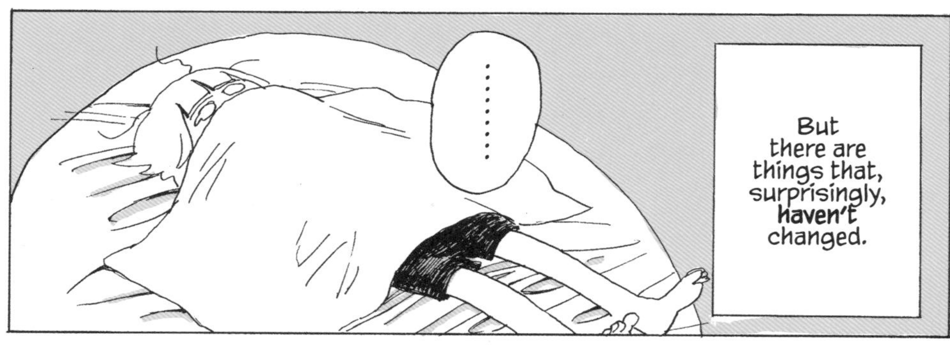
……
But there are things that, surprisingly, **haven't** changed.

Like the fact that I can still feel so sad, miserable, and lonely that I sometimes burst into tears.
WAA AA AAAH!
COLIC AND NIGHT CRYING HIXXKIOGAN MEDICINE HELPS BABIES SLEEP THROUGH THE NIGHT!

I've cried mainly because...
WAAAAA AAAH!
I'VE BEEN ALIVE FOR TWENTY-NINE YEARS, AND I'VE NEVER HAD A SINGLE LOVE!!

And...
WHEN I THINK ABOUT IT, I'VE NEVER EVEN KISSED OR HAD SEX WITH SOMEONE I LIKED WHO LIKED ME BACK!!!!
GAH!
DUN
DUUUN

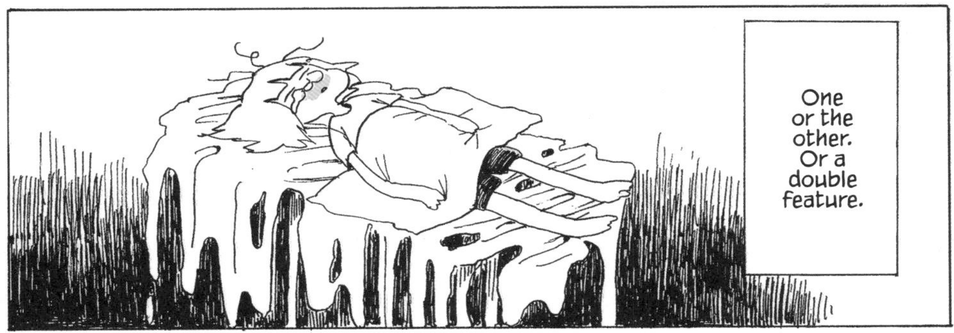
One or the other. Or a double feature.

When I realized this so abruptly, it felt like falling into a bottomless pit.

I couldn't breathe, and my chest hurt--literally.

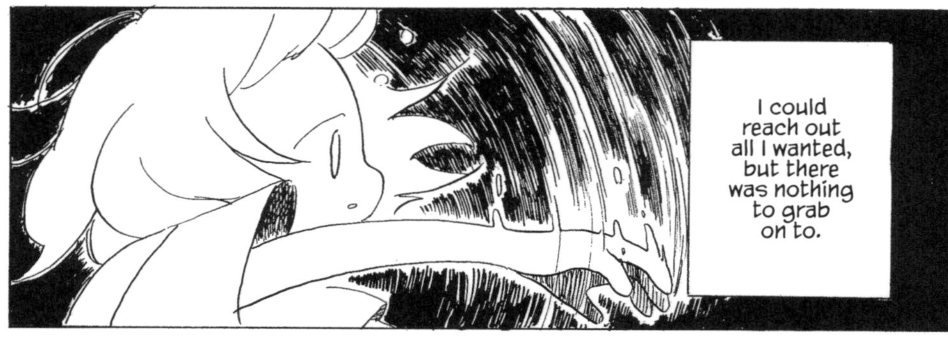
I could reach out all I wanted, but there was nothing to grab on to.

Maybe the closest comparison to that feeling...

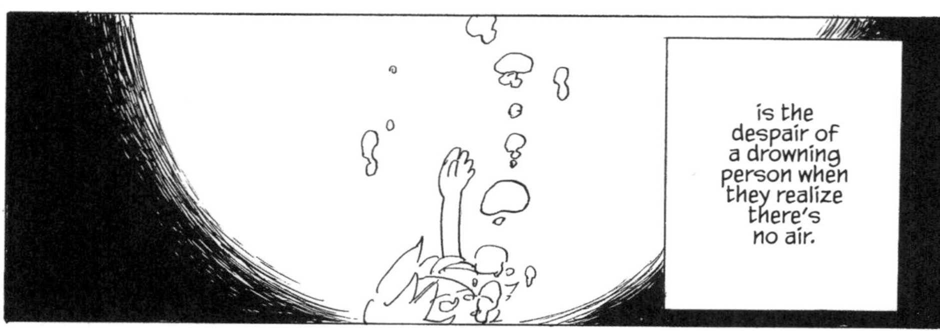
is the despair of a drowning person when they realize there's no air.

I'M CONSTANTLY SORRY ABOUT THIS, NEIGHBORS! WAAAH!!
UNNNH, I'M SO SAD. THIS IS SO HARD, I'M SO LONELY!
UNNNNH...

I WANT TO LOVE AND BE *LOOOVED* !!!!

......?!
I'VE NEVER HAD THAT THOUGHT BEFORE. I WANT TO LOVE AND BE LOVED...?
A THIRTYISH WOMAN LIVING ALONE AND CRYING ABOUT *THAT?!* THERE'S NO TWIST--THAT'S ALL IT IS! I HATE IT!

THAT REMINDS ME. I FEEL LIKE I'VE STOPPED THINKING SO MUCH ABOUT DEATH, AND NOW I'M THINKING ABOUT THIS, INSTEAD...
HONK HONK HONK

The energy that, until now, had swelled up in the space between life and death...
DEATH
ENERGY
LIFE
turned toward a thirst for love.
LOVE
ENERGY

MY FACE IS ALL BLOTCHY AND I CAN'T BREATHE.
plap
plap
I DON'T KNOW IF IT'LL HELP, BUT I'LL PUT A COLD COMPRESS ON.

IT HURTS. I'M SAD. IT'S HARD.
SNIFFLE SNIFFLE SNIFFLE

DING-DOOONG DING-DOOONG
HUH?

YES?
KA-CHAK
I'M HERE TO DELIVER YOUR FRIDGE.
OH, RIGHT. I'M GLAD I GOT UP.

HUP!
IT'LL GET COLD IN ABOUT TWO HOURS.
SIGN HERE, PLEASE.
SURE.

YOU'VE... GOT A FEVER?
ARE YOU OKAY?

....?
......!

OH! YES!
ALL RIGHT, THEN. THANK YOU!

KA-TUNK
....

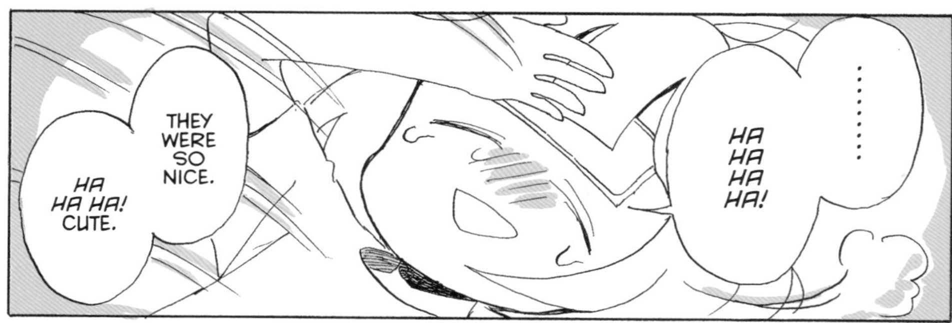
....
HA HA HA HA!
THEY WERE SO NICE.
HA HA HA! CUTE.

The sad things, the painful things, the hard things...
and the happy things. It felt really great to do it all myself. **All** of it was mine alone.

Living by myself is fun.
Please continue doing this-- and grow so you can have more fun encounters in the future.

My
Solo
Exchange
Diary

Dear Nagata Kabi... This is Nagata Kabi.
Um, is it okay if I talk about my mom again?

IT'S LIKE...MY HEART'S BEEN BROKEN.
ALTHOUGH I'VE NEVER DATED ANYONE, SO I DON'T ACTUALLY KNOW.

MOM DOESN'T SMILE FOR ME THE WAY SHE USED TO.
I FELT **SECURE** WHEN SHE SMILED.
I SAID I WANTED HER TO BE HAPPY OR WHATEVER, BUT I REALLY JUST WANTED HER TO SMILE.

THE MOM WHO BABIED ME IS GONE NOW.
I'LL NEVER SEE HER AGAIN.

I'M SURE THERE WERE DAYS WHEN WE LOVED EACH OTHER.
OR WAS THAT LOVE JUST AN **ILLUSION...?**

Here's a rough overview of me now.
THINGS I IGNORED WHILE AT MY PARENTS' HOUSE ARE ERUPTING.
FEELS LIKE A BIG HOLE HAS OPENED UP.
THE THING I'VE ALWAYS WANTED IS RIGHT IN FRONT OF ME, BUT I CAN'T TAKE IT.

......
I don't even know anymore. To sum up: I'm sad.

AHHH...
I EXPECTED TOO MUCH.

I wanted to recover with a warm word and some kindness from my family, and I expected too much.
TEN YEARS AGO, I READ THAT SORT OF THING A LOT IN STORIES ABOUT RECOVERING FROM EATING DISORDERS.
I HAVEN'T SEEN IT LATELY, THOUGH.
I mean, I thought my family loved me.
AWW
YOU GUYS!

When I complained to people about living with my parents...
THEY JUST NAG AND TREAT ME LIKE A LITTLE KID! I HATE IT!
EVERY MOVE I MAKE, I FEEL LIKE THEY'RE WATCHING ME AND COMMENTING ON IT!

YOUR PARENTS CARE DEEPLY ABOUT YOU.
THEY LOVE YOU MORE THAN ANYTHING.
That's what I was told, anyway.

I thought that the bad stuff and the rigidity meant that my family loved me.

Fortunately, I never had to deal with violence or separation or poverty. (I really am thankful for that.)

So, I thought I had no right to be struggling or in pain.

I basically ignored it, but still-- it really was hard. It really *did* hurt.

CUTE! I'M SO HAPPY!
......
NEWS
HOW AWFUL!!
?
Even faced with the same event, positive or negative reactions differ from person to person. It's all subjective.

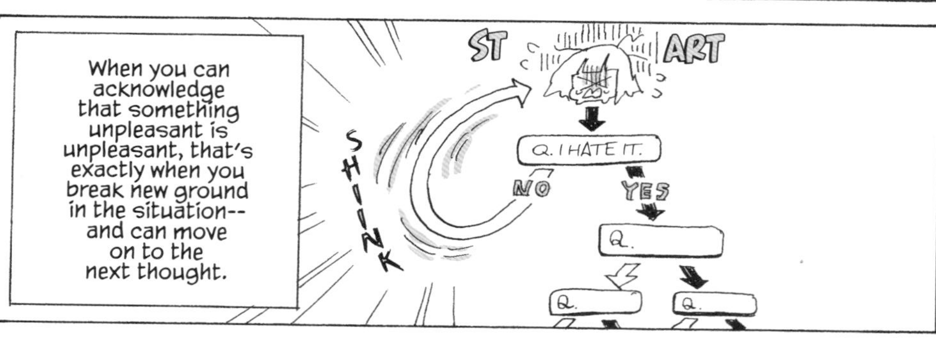
When you can acknowledge that something unpleasant is unpleasant, that's exactly when you break new ground in the situation--and can move on to the next thought.
SHUNK
START
Q. I HATE IT.
NO
YES
Q.
Q.
Q.

......
BUT YOU REALLY LOVE ME WITH ALL YOUR HEART, RIGHT?
I came to realize this in recent years. It exacerbated my unhappiness with my family, but I still expected them to love me.

Now that I'm away from them, I can think it without fear.
THERE WAS NO LOVE...
BETWEEN ANY OF US.

We're a small group in the shape of a family.

I moved out, but I sometimes go back home on some errand.

Well, now that I think about it... I assigned too many roles to my mother.

An independent person would have a bunch of different people to turn to, but I loaded everything onto my mother.

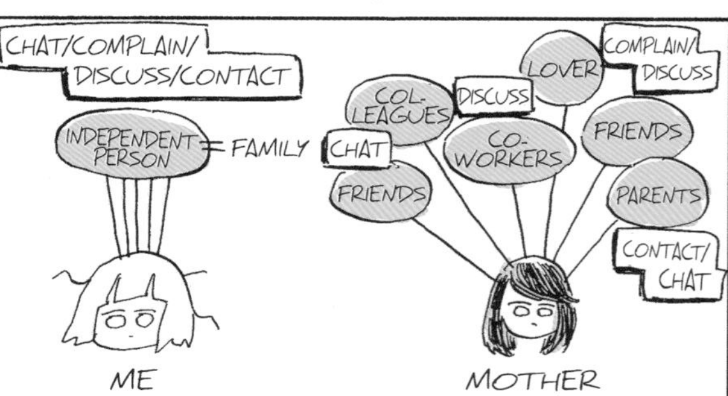

It ended up being this thing where I ranted to my mother about problems with my mother. (Sorry.)

That was cut off now, so a hole popped open. I was just barely connected to other people by my work.

I REALLY DO HAVE TO GET MORE PEOPLE TO RELY ON!
WORK
MORE PEOPLE, FEWER EXPECTATIONS OF EACH OF THEM!!
IN OTHER WORDS, INDEPENDENCE!!!

I'VE SAID IT BEFORE, I'LL SAY IT AGAIN-- I'M STILL NOT INDEPENDENT!!
INDEPEN DENCE
DAMMIT! THIS TIME, I'LL GET THERE FOR SURE!!

SO... WHAT CONCRETE THINGS CAN I DO TO MOVE TOWARD THAT?
PROBABLY START WITH JUST MEETING PEOPLE.
I NEVER SEE ANYONE, AFTER ALL.

I REALLY DON'T DO SOCIAL STUFF...
LIKE LOOKING AT SOMETHING WITH ANOTHER PERSON SO WE CAN SHARE AN EMOTION OVER IT.

HM. I SHOULD PROBABLY WATCH MORE MOVIES OR ANIME OR SOMETHING.
AND READ MORE BOOKS AND MANGA.

THEN I COULD TALK TO PEOPLE ABOUT THEM.
DID YOU SEE XX?
I DID!
OPINIONS
I COULD MAKE THAT HAPPEN RIGHT AWAY, ACTUALLY-- I COULD WRITE MY OPINIONS ON TWITTER AND STUFF. CAN'T *THAT* BE A START TO CONVERSATIONS?

I basically never meet up with people outside of work. I haven't seen a movie in five years.
I'VE ONLY GOT A SMART PHONE.
I don't buy books or manga-- I don't have a TV or computer, either.

I NEED TO CHANGE ALL THAT!
THIS WOULD BE AN INVESTMENT IN TAKING CARE OF MYSELF. I SHOULD DEFINITELY DO IT.

And then, someday, I wanna meet someone... where we both know we'll become precious to each other.

It probably won't happen right away, but...

Please work hard to get love from someone other than Mom!!

My
Solo
Exchange
Diary

My
Solo
Exchange
Diary

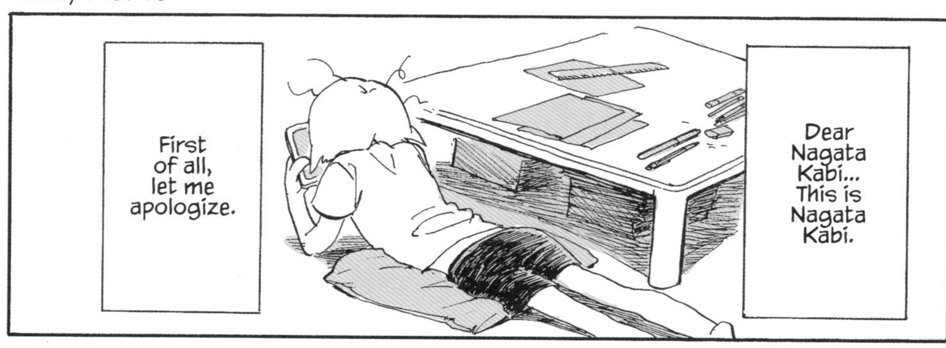

a watch thread on a massive online bulletin board. (FYI, a watch thread is a thread that keeps an eye on and discusses something.)

NAGATA KABI WATCH THR
[FORBIDDEN]
000: ANONYMOUS @
ID: 00000(1)
000: ANONYMOUS @

Maybe because I was searching for myself on Twitter, I wasn't getting any *really* negative opinions.

And that's where I found it: a captivating world where people did nothing but observe and discuss me!!

They weren't just treating my **work** as interesting content, but also my life, my words. There was something appealing about that.

And then I made the dumb move of using Twitter to answer questions that came up in the watch thread (my most regretted action of the year).

So...when I drew my thoughts or stuff that had happened to me, I'd be told, "Don't draw that." And if I **didn't** draw those things, people would say, "Don't hide the bad stuff."

SILENT...
WOO!
When I was in junior high, I hid myself so I wouldn't stand out.

When I went home, I felt like my classmates were watching me from somewhere, laughing as they saw how different I was in my house.

I felt that way back in my parents' house during my part-timer days, too--when they watched and commented on every little thing I did.
STILL HAVEN'T SAID ANYTHING.
THEY'LL THINK THIS ABOUT THAT.
THEY'LL THINK THAT ABOUT THIS...

IT'S HAPPENING AGAIN!
I FOUGHT TO GET MY OWN PLACE, BUT WHAT WAS THE POINT IF I DO THIS AGAIN?!
I HAVE TO STOP LOOKING!!

NOT FOR ANYONE'S BENEFIT.
MISDIRECTED EFFORTS, CONSIDERATION, AND SELF-RESTRAINT.
This was bad because all my efforts and consideration and self-restraint were misdirected, and it wasn't actually for anyone's benefit.

AH!
MAYBE I'LL DRAW THAT FOR THEM.
AND YET, STILL LOOKING.
IT'S NOT THAT I *WASN'T* SAYING THAT.
I MEAN, IF YOU'RE GONNA JUMP TO THE CONCLUSION THAT I REALLY THINK LIKE THIS, IT'LL END UP BEING AN ENDLESS ARGUMENT WHEN I DISAGREE...

I JUST...
I HATE **THEM** DECIDING WHAT *I* THINK.
YOU'RE THINKING XX.
GRAND-MA
YOU REALLY THINK XX, RIGHT?
MOM
ENOUGH. HUSH.
DAD

FOR CRYING OUT LOUD!
THAT'S WHY I TOLD YOU TO *STOP LOOKING!!*
STOP *LOOOO-OOKING* !!!

I think that being *this* concerned with what other people think of me...

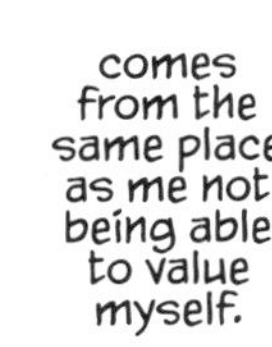

comes from the same place as me not being able to value myself.

I have no personal measuring stick.

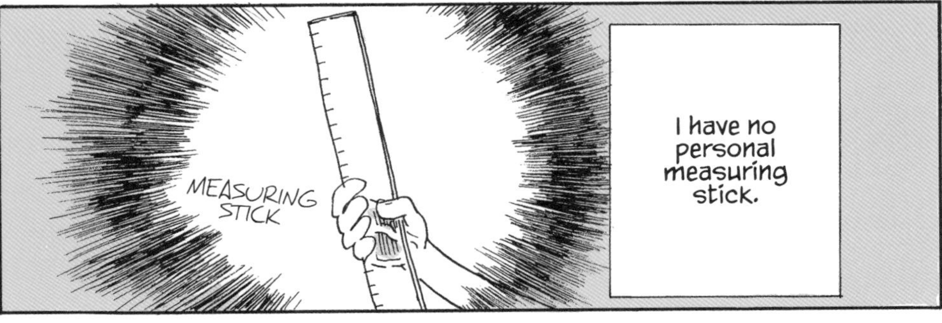

Without that personal measuring stick, how can you assess yourself? You don't know your own pace or growth on the scale of what you're capable of. It drags down your ability to self-evaluate.

Someone without that personal measuring stick is anxious about whether they have enough value to even be allowed to live.

But since you don't have the tool to measure yourself against yourself, you compare yourself to other people.

even when you're just comparing the size of stuff you can see, the scale is different for different people. It's pointless.
THEY ARE LOWER THAN ME...
PHEW!
ACTUALLY 10
ACTUALLY 6
When you do that...

ISN'T THIS THAT THING WHERE I'M HYPER-AWARE OF OTHER PEOPLE, COMPARE MYSELF TO THEM, AND THEN GET JEALOUS?!
BECAUSE I DON'T HAVE MY OWN MEASURING STICK!!
HANDKER-CHIEF

MY MEASURING STICK
PUT OUT A BOOK
NO ACTUAL RESULTS OF ANY KIND
I couldn't be happy about my book launch and its positive reception, but that **would've** made me happy if I'd had my own measuring stick.

I measured myself with my parents' measuring stick and waited for them to assign me my value.
MEASURE ME!!
AND GIVE ME A GOOD NUMBER!!

What exactly is this "measuring stick," then?
HMMM...
"SELF-ESTEEM"?
THAT MIGHT BE THE CLOSEST.

IF YOU HAVE SELF-ESTEEM...
SELF-ESTEEM = PERSONAL MEASURING STICK

SELF-ESTEEM UP!
2016
2015
GROWTH
YOU CAN UNDERSTAND YOUR OWN GROWTH...
AND YOU CAN RAISE YOUR SELF-ESTEEM TO GREATER HEIGHTS.

THEN THERE'S NO INCESSANT COMPARING YOURSELF TO SOMEONE ELSE, OR GETTING JEALOUS OR ANXIOUS...
I...
I WANT THAT...!!

Even still, the opinions I saw in that brief period nagged at me for a long time.

Before *My Lesbian Experience with Loneliness* officially went on sale, I was stunned that everyone I showed it to, including my parents, was apparently shocked by the homosexuality and the escort agency, but...

That was an issue, sure. But also, maybe...
BUT THAT WASN'T THE *POINT* OF THE BOOK?!
THEY CAN READ IT HOWEVER THEY WAAANT!

I'VE GOT MY OWN PREJUDICE ABOUT HOMOSEXUALITY AND ESCORT AGENCIES...
AND THAT'S WHY I WAS SO SHOCKED?

BECAUSE I UNDERSTAND THAT PREJUDICE, I KNOW HOW MY RELATIVES ARE LOOKING AT ME NOW, AND THAT'S A SHOCK.
SO, ISN'T IT THAT I REALLY WANTED TO REJECT ALL THAT AND RUN AWAY?

Maybe I'm hurting other people, including the women at that agency, without even knowing it. Maybe I'll **keep** doing that.

It felt like I needed self-esteem and that personal measuring stick so I wouldn't just waste away--so I could keep drawing while being aware every time that it happened.

And then, I'll do lots of (legal) fun stuff that my parents and people with different values will probably rail against.

My
Solo
Exchange
Diary

This is Nagata Kabi.
OKAY!
I'M STILL AT OO.
Dear Nagata Kabi...

And...
Compared to when this series began, I'm seeing more people than ever.

FOR SURE.
WHAT?! REALLY?!!

I'LL SEND YOU AN INVITATION~!
WHAT'S YOUR ADDRESS?
THIS IS THE FIRST TIME IN MY ENTIRE LIFE...
THAT I'VE BEEN INVITED TO A FRIEND'S WEDDING.

It had already been about a year since my friend signed the marriage license...
GULP GULP
LET'S SEE HERE.
but inside me, "marriage" and "happiness" were still really tied together.

She'd always been cute and pretty.
But now her face and aura gleamed even more, almost like she was a different person.

This might be a weird way of putting it, but you use marriage to trick yourself into being happy. (I think?)
HUSBAND
MARRIAGE
HEE HEE! TAKE THAT!
It's reliable, refreshing, and joyful.

"Loving and being loved" is an incredible thing, huh...?
GLEAM
AH! IT'S BLINDING!

Even if they had invited me, I know I would've disappointed them and made them hate me. I was scared and embarrassed and pathetic, and I would've turned them down.

And I've had friends before. Was it just that they couldn't *actually* talk to me?

I wrote about this earlier--that I couldn't accept the positive reactions when I finally got the book out.

But I've discovered lately that I *did* take them to heart, without even realizing it.

All the positive comments had become a support for me at some point and that made it so I wasn't too afraid or pathetic to see people.

CAN WE BE FRIENDS...

AND IF THAT GOES WELL, MAYBE START **DATING?**

After twenty-nine years of history, something finally shifted.

She'd realized she liked women a few years earlier and was looking for a girlfriend.

HER

I'M CURRENTLY FREE, SO GOING TO A HOTEL OR SOMETHING IS TOTALLY FINE, BUT I GUESS YOU'D PROBABLY HATE THAT?

H-H-H...
H-H-H-H-
HOTEL!!!!
HOTEL
!!!!

THE KIND OF SEXUAL ACT WHERE YOU DON'T PAY MONEY OR RESERVE A TIME...?!!

The door to a world still unknown to me...
KREEEEEEEEEE
had finally opened!!

Everyone(?), I'm sorry. I'm not gonna be an old amateur virgin anymore.

I had nothing but ulterior motives.

I'D ACTUALLY LOVE TO MEET YOU RIGHT NOW, BUT I'M ON MY PERIOD. THE END OF THIS WEEK SHOULD BE GOOD, THOUGH...!

I COULD MEET UP WITH YOU TOMORROW AFTER WORK, IF YOU WANT TO TALK A LITTLE.

This was all so new to me.

*A famous gay neighborhood in Tokyo, where a variety of gay bars, shops, and services can be found.

YOU WROTE IN YOUR MANGA THAT YOU WANTED TO DATE SOMEONE IN STAGES.
IN ENTRY NO. 2.
IS DOING SOMETHING SUDDEN LIKE THIS REALLY OKAY?

!!
Y-YEAH...
I HADN'T THOUGHT ANYTHING THROUGH.

SH-SHE'S BEING SO SINCERE WITH ME?
SHE'S USING HER WORDS AND REALLY TALKING TO MEEE?!

WE'LL BE CLOSING SOON.
THANK YOU FOR YOUR PATRONAGE.
WHAT TIME IS THE LAST TRAIN AGAIN?
OH!
UM!

I'LL PAY FOR YOUR TAXI.
SO, WILL YOU STAY JUST A LITTLE LONGER?

O-OKAY...
HUH? I DON'T... KNOW WHAT THIS IS. I DON'T GET ANYTHING ANYMORE.

THE LAST TRAIN'S REALLY GONNA LEAVE SOON...
We looked for a twenty-four-hour place where we could sit.

OH!
UH...
CONVENIENCE
JUST LET ME GRAB A DRINK.
We stopped by a convenience store, and I drank by myself.

Then we settled down on a nearby bench.
GIRLS I LIKE ALWAYS MANAGE TO GET A GIRLFRIEND *RIGHT THEN.*
IT'S HAPPENED TO ME THREE TIMES IN A ROW, NOW.
THEN MAYBE I'LL GET A GIRLFRIEND, TOO.

IF THERE'S SOMEONE ELSE IN YOUR LIFE WHO'S GOOD TO YOU, NAGATA-SAN, THAT'S A GOOD THING.
IF YOU THINK OF ME AS A FRIEND, WE CAN BE FRIENDS. IF YOU THINK OF ME AS A LOVER, THEN I THINK IT WOULD BE GREAT TO BE YOUR LOVER.

SO, WELL... IF IT'S OKAY WITH YOU...
CAN WE BE FRIENDS...
AND IF THAT GOES WELL, MAYBE START **DATING?**

—
?!!
DRUNK
IF THIS WAS AN ARRANGED MARRIAGE MEETING WITH PARENTS, IT WOULD GET SETTLED IMMEDIATELY.
BY THE WAY, YOU CAN DRAW THIS IN YOUR MANGA, IF YOU WANT.
WHAT ?!
※ I GOT PERMISSION AGAIN AT THE THUMBNAILS STAGE.

WE WENT ALL NIGHT, DIDN'T WE?
SECOND ONE
IT'S... TOTALLY MORNING.

MAY I TAKE...
YOUR HAND?
SQUEEZE

It was strange.
The sensation that she liked me radiated through the air, her voice, her skin.

UM... IF...
IF YOU'RE OKAY DOING IT WITH SOMEONE YOU'RE NOT DATING...

CAN I...
KISS YOU, JUST ONCE?

......
YOU WANT TO DO THAT *HERE?*
YES.

kiss

PLIP

My heart was full of something I didn't know.

We went our separate ways in the early morning, after agreeing to see each other again soon.

Please let me keep telling this story a little while longer.
THAT'S THE FIRST TIME I'VE EVER KISSED SOMEONE I LIKE.

My
Solo
Exchange
Diary

We decided on a second meeting a week later.
HER
YAY! A DATE WITH OO-SAN (REAL NAME)!
D- D-D... D-D-DATE?!!!

DATE.
HOTEL
HOTEL
DA
DAA!
CAT CAFE

DATE.
WHAT DOES ONE DO ON A DATE?
WHAT MAKES SOMETHING A DATE...?
WHAT CONDITIONS MUST BE FULFILLED TO DEFINE A SITUATION AS "A DATE"?

!

OH!
OH.

I DON'T... GET THAT HAPPY A LOOK ON MY FACE...
IT'S ALREADY BEEN A WEEEEK!

BECAUSE I DON'T LIKE HER ENOUGH...?

SOMETIMES YOU DON'T SAY NO WHEN SOMEONE ASKS YOU OUT, BUT IT'S NOT ACTUALLY TWO-SIDED LOVE, RIGHT?! EVERYONE, WHAT SHOULD I DO?!
I DON'T KNOW ...!!
STARE
CLUMP OF FOUN-DATION
......
WERE YOU IN A RUSH WITH YOUR MAKE-UP?

I'd taken a bath and put on make-up, which I normally didn't do, because I had an ulterior motive.

I thought my heart would be filled if I had contact (especially the intimate kind) with someone who liked me.

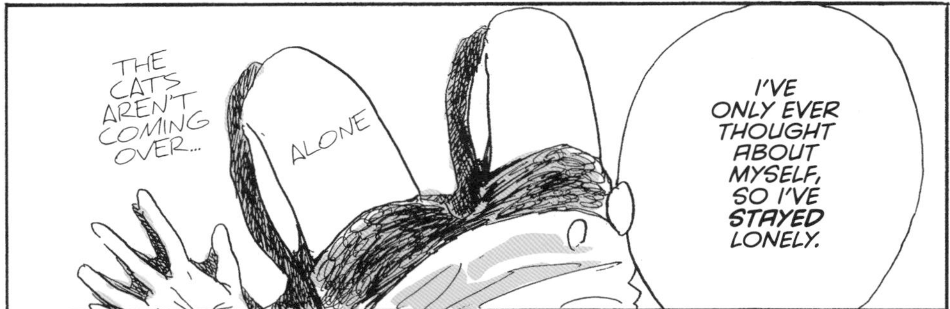

Right.
I'd thought
all I needed was
someone to turn
that feeling of
"like" toward me,
and I'd be happy...
but I was wrong.

If you don't have respect, admiration, and trust-- good stuff like that...
for each other...

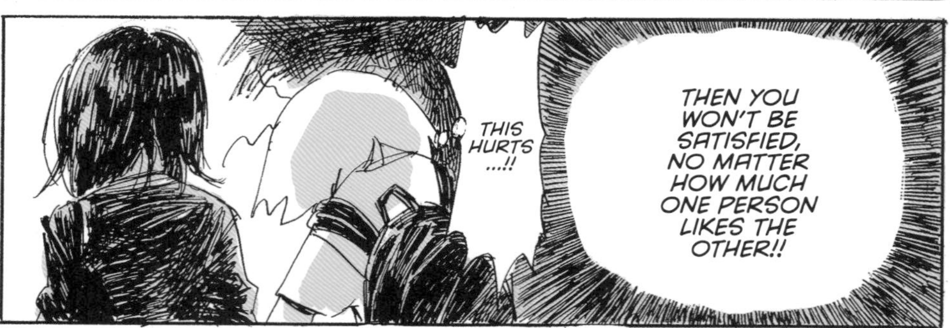
THEN YOU WON'T BE SATISFIED, NO MATTER HOW MUCH ONE PERSON LIKES THE OTHER!!
THIS HURTS ...!!

WHERE DO YOU WANT TO GO AFTER THIS?
HMMM.
UNTIL TODAY, I WAS RARING TO GO TO A HOTEL.

BUT UNLESS I'M THINKING WAY MORE ABOUT HER, I KNOW GOING TO A HOTEL WON'T SATISFY MY HEART.
THE LESBIAN BARS IN DOYAMA DON'T OPEN UNTIL EVENING...
SO WE STILL HAVE SOME TIME.

FAMILY RESTAURANT.
YOU GOT ALCOHOL *AND* THE UNLIMITED NON-ALCOHOLIC DRINKS, *HM?*
MY USUAL STYLE.
YES...

19:00
UM, I'M ACTUALLY RUNNING UP AGAINST A DEADLINE.
I SHOULD BE GETTING HOME, SO I'M GONNA PASS ON DOYAMA THIS TIME.

OH.
SLUMP
ER, MAYBE THIS IS A LITTLE SELFISH, BUT...
YOU WON'T KNOW WHAT'S GOING ON IN MY HEAD UNLESS I SAY IT, SO I'LL SAY IT.

UM!
CAN I BE WITH YOU FOR JUST ANOTHER HALF AN HOUR?!

THE TRUTH IS, I...
I REALLY WANT TO SEE YOU HOME!!
I WANT TO BE TOGETHER, EVEN FOR JUST A MINUTE LONGER.
I'D EVEN BE HAPPY TO COME CLEAN YOUR APARTMENT, IF YOU WANT.
I CAN'T BELIEVE...

YOU CAN LIKE A PERSON THIS MUCH... AND STILL NOT HAVE THEM LIKE YOU BACK THE SAME WAY.

I FINALLY HAVE SOMEONE WHO LIKES ME. I'M SORRY FOR BEING SO OUT OF IT.
tousle tousle
I'M SORRY I CAN'T GIVE YOU WHAT YOU WANT.

I FINALLY MET SOMEONE WHO THINKS LIKE THIS ABOUT ME...
BUT I'M NOT CONSIDERATE OR RESPECTFUL OF OTHER PEOPLE... SO I'M STILL LONELY.

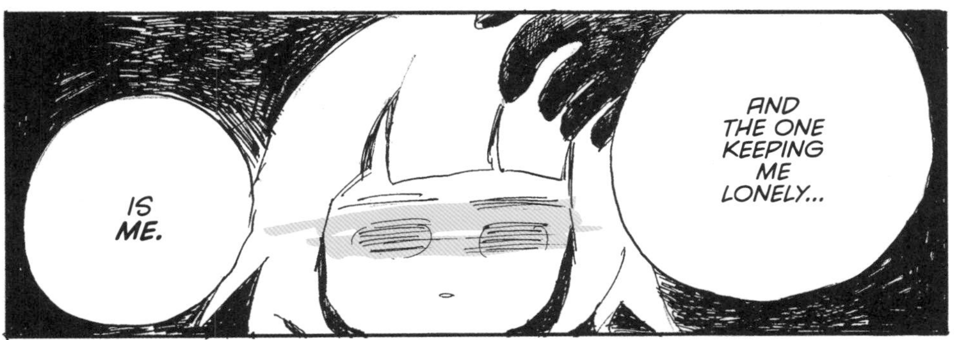
AND THE ONE KEEPING ME LONELY...
IS ME.

TICKET GATE
I REALLY DO WANT TO SEE YOUR PLACE...!!
OH! YOU DON'T LOOK VERY SURE... I GUESS I SHOULD STOP, HUH?

STAGGER
IT'S FUTILE...
"LOVING AND BEING LOVED" IS LIKE A MIRACLE.
STAGGER

CH-CLNK
NEXT STOP, OO... NEXT STOP, OO...
GULP
GULP
ALCOHOL
Dear Nagata Kabi... This is Nagata Kabi.
CHA-CLANK

You've been through a bewildering few months.
NICE WORK. AND GIMME A SIP!
PAT
ALCOHOL

Your book came out.
Your dream of living by yourself came true.

You're paying the rent, the utilities, and all daily expenses with your own income.
ATM
M-MY BALAAAANCE!!!

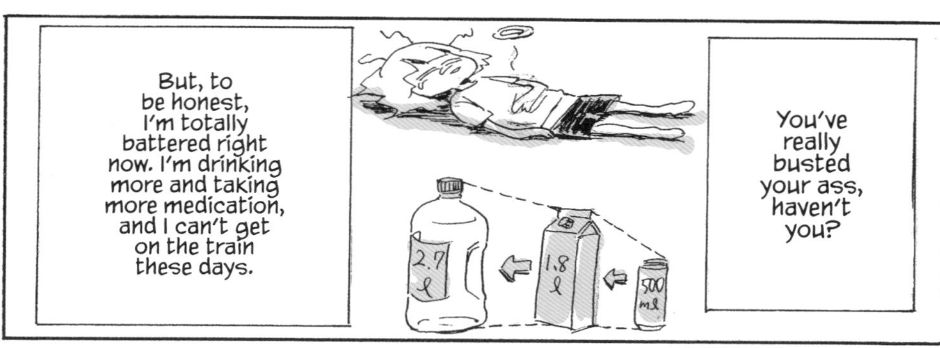
You've really busted your ass, haven't you?
But, to be honest, I'm totally battered right now. I'm drinking more and taking more medication, and I can't get on the train these days.
2.7 l
1.8 l
500 ml

Once, when I stopped caring about the future, I cut my neck with kitchen scissors-- but it turns out the carotid artery is on the *inside* of your neck muscles. Those muscles hurt for a long time after that.

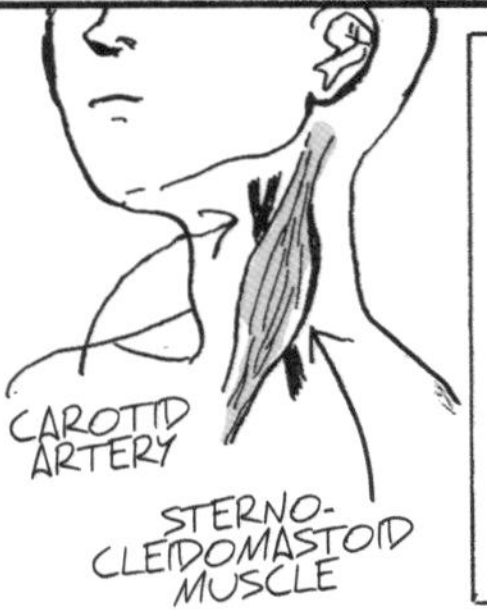

I've seriously thought, a bunch of times, that I can't do these strips any longer.

I don't know what my mom or dad or anyone else is saying...

From now on, I'm fine with getting hurt again, so please don't give up.

but you've really worked hard and have grown so much for me.

And please make sure to get that "loving and being loved" thing.

Please do your job well!

My Solo Exchange Diary, Vol. 1 | END

My
Solo
Exchange
Diary

First published on HiBaNa's pixiv Comic page (https://comic.pixiv.net/magazines/131)
Collects chapters from 5/23, 5/30, 6/13, 6/27, 7/11, 7/25, 8/8, 8/22, 9/12, 9/26, 10/24, and 10/31.

~Bonus Entry~
SO, I GUESS YOU'RE WONDERING HOW THINGS WENT AFTER THAT.
HRFF.
AND THEN NO. 12 HAPPENED.
AFTER ENTRY NO. 11, I GOT COMMENTS LIKE: "CONGRATULATIONS!!"

WHAT *IS* THIS?
WE DIDN'T SPLIT, WE'RE NOT JOINED AT THE HIP...
THINGS DIDN'T GO ANYWHERE.

TALKING WITH MY EDITOR ON THE PHONE.
RIGHT, I SHOULD.
PLEASE MAKE SURE YOU DOUBLE-CHECK WITH HER.
IN YOUR MANGA
YOU CAN DRAW ME...
IT'S A SENSITIVE TOPIC, AND IT'LL LINGER IN BOOK FORM.

COULD YOU TAKE A LOOK AT THE THUMBNAILS?
ATTACHED FILE
IT'S NOT REALLY A GREAT STORY FOR HER, HUH...?

*The kanji for "busy (忙)" is written with the characters for "heart/mind (心)" and "lose (亡)."

OH...

I DID SOMETHING AWFUL.

I FOUND A WAY OF SURVIVING IN NON-FICTION.
I WAS ONLY THINKING ABOUT **MYSELF.**
BUT IF I'M GONNA BE *JUST FINE* WITH HURTING PEOPLE...
I'LL NEVER FIND MUTUAL LOVE.
NO WAY.
Dear Nagata Kabi... This is Nagata Kabi.
Despite everything, I still know that someday... you'll love and be loved.
BUT WITH WHO?!

SEVEN SEAS ENTERTAINMENT PRE[...]

My Solo Exchange Diary Volume 1

(true) story & art by NAGATA KABI

TRANSLATION
Jocelyne Allen

ADAPTATION
Lianne Sentar

LETTERING AND LAYOUT
Karis Page

LOGO DESIGN
KC Fabellon

ORIGINAL DESIGN
Yasuhisa Kawatani
(Kawatani Design)

COVER DESIGN
Nicky Lim

PROOFREADER
Shanti Whitesides
Danielle King

ASSISTANT EDITOR
Jenn Grunigen

PRODUCTION ASSISTANT
CK Russell

PRODUCTION MANAGER
Lissa Pattillo

EDITOR-IN-CHIEF
Adam Arnold

PUBLISHER
Jason DeAngelis

HITORI KOKAN NIKKI VOL.1
by Nagata Kabi

Original Japanese edition published by SHOGAKUKAN.
English translation rights in the United States of America, Canada, and the United Kingdom arranged with SHOGAKUKAN through Tuttle-Mori Agency, Inc.

ISBN: 978-1-626928-89-3

Printed in Canada

First Printing: June 2018

10 9 8 7 6 5 4 3 2 1

FOLLOW US ONLINE: ***www.sevenseasentertainment.com***

READING DIRECTIONS

This book reads from ***right to left***, Japanese style. If this is your first time reading manga, you start reading from the top right panel on each page and take it from there. If you get lost, just follow the numbered diagram here. It may seem backwards at first, but you'll get the hang of it! Have fun!!

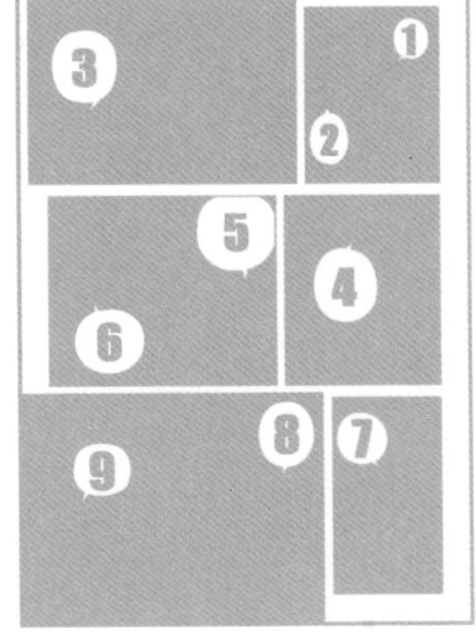